Rum Tales

Down Home Yarns
Around a Pot-Bellied Stove

David Mossman

Pottersfield Press
Lawrencetown Beach, Nova Scotia, Canada

Library and Archives Canada Cataloguing in Publication

Title: Rum tales : down home yarns around a pot-bellied stove / David Mossman.
Names: Mossman, David, author.
Identifiers: Canadiana (print) 20200172778 | Canadiana (ebook) 20200172824 | ISBN 9781989725092 (softcover) | ISBN 9781989725108 (HTML)
Subjects: LCSH: Lunenburg (N.S. : County)—History—20th century. | LCSH: Lunenburg (N.S. : County)— Social life and customs—20th century. | LCSH: Lunenburg (N.S. : County)—Biography.
Classification: LCC FC2345.L85 M57 2020 | DDC 971.6/23—dc23

Cover design: Gail LeBlanc

Pottersfield Press gratefully acknowledges the financial support of the Government of Canada for our publishing activities. We also acknowledge the support of the Canada Council for the Arts and the Province of Nova Scotia which has assisted us to develop and promote our creative industries for the benefit of all Nova Scotians.

Pottersfield Press
248 Leslie Road
East Lawrencetown, Nova Scotia, Canada, B2Z 1T4
Website: www.PottersfieldPress.com
To order, phone 1-800-NIMBUS9 (1-800-646-2879) www.nimbus.ns.ca

Printed in Canada

Pottersfield Press is committed to protecting our natural environment. This book is made of material from well-managed FSC®-certified forests and other controlled sources.

Dedicated to Pauline Marjorie Kariler

It is funny, but it strikes me that a person without anecdotes that they nurse while they live, and that survive them, are more likely to be utterly lost not only to history but the family following them. Of course this is the fate of most souls, reducing entire lives, no matter how vivid and wonderful, to those sad black names on withering family trees, with half a date dangling after and a question mark.

– Sebastian Barry, *The Secret Scripture*

Contents

Dramatis Personae

Aubrey Leon Backman

Carmen Creaser

Amos Crouse

Leroy (Roy) Henry Deal

Douglas Thomas Himmelman

Timothy Haliburton (Bertie) Himmelman

Willy Kaizer

Charles (William) Leary

Arthur Benjamin (AB) Lohnes

Kenneth Lohnes

David Lawrence Mawhinney

Maxwell Mosher

Lawrence (Laurie) Winwood Mossman

Titus Milton Mossman

Austin Wamboldt

Frank Zinck

Prologue

The stories in this book provide a taste of life during the first half of the twentieth century in the small fishing village of Rose Bay, Lunenburg County, Nova Scotia.

The history (circa 1919 to 1958) reflected in these stories is akin to a voyage under sail in Maritime coastal waters – turbulent and thick o' fog in places, with boundaries blurred between fact and fiction. Outside of cultures with a tradition of oral history, human memory in monumental form is exceeding rare. At best, it may last three generations, yet even then there is a natural tendency to revise our recollections. No matter how long stuck in storage, most memories go missing in the transition to anonymity. Memories of those travellers are texts taken to the grave – irretrievable. No effort is required to lose an ancestor or their stories.

As narrator, my first line of defense is that many of these stories are taken from libraries no longer in existence – pieced together from old tape recordings. I had spoken with Max Mosher, Douglas Himmelman, and David L. Mawhinney; Ralph Getson interviewed Amos Crouse and Aubrey Backman, while Carmen Creaser chatted with Laurie Meister. Distance from the shore of truth, at least in these cases, ought to be minimal. In only one instance is a name changed for confidentiality.

Most of the stories are selective in details or biased or slanted to some extent. Although I was not around during the Governor General's visit to my hometown in 1923, local write-ups and the intimacy of my elders with those times promote my recall. The story of *Andrava*'s survival during the August gale of 1927 is taken from Captain Rollie Knickle's verbatim account and compared with that of doryman Roy Deal, portions of which in later years I heard from Roy. In sum, most of the dialogue is in the realm of historical fiction, created from memory, as close to real life as possible.

Arthur Benjamin (AB) Lohnes's General Store in Rose Bay is a classic example from the halcyon days of country stores in Lunenburg County. The village is an integral part of Riverport and District as detailed in my books *Oceans of Rum: The Nova Scotia Banana Fleet in Rum-Runner Heaven* and *The Legend of Gladee's Canteen: Down Home on a Nova Scotia Beach*. Little now remains of AB's store except a dilapidated shack. Singularly unimpressive, it crouches low on the south bank of what every young fisherman in the village knows as Arthur's Brook, at the foot of the hill below the Crossroads in Upper Rose Bay. For nearly half a century Arthur's store was known to his family as The Shop, and throughout the wider community as AB's.

Country general stores in the Maritimes, as throughout the nation, are now largely supplanted by corporations whose grasp extends over and beyond the Western world. Back in AB's day, stores like his supplied not only villagers' basic material needs of food and clothing, but also important social services. Like a church – and there were three within sight – AB's store was part of an important nameless franchise, in effect a competing institution of sorts.

AB's daughter, Margaret Jean, provided me with key insights into her father's behaviour and philosophy of life. A childhood friend of my sister, she wrote to me applauding the publication of my first book *Going Over: A Nova Scotian Soldier in World War I* – the story of my father Titus Mossman. From there, we two resolved to set *Rum Tales* in her father's store, which is totally appropriate given that those tales once resounded off the walls of that simple shelter. Thus the course of the narrative evolved.

These days, loafing gets a bad rap as an idle way of passing time. However, quite apart from its material purpose, The Shop provided a place where, with the blessing of their wives, men could relax and share their worries of the day. What harm could possibly come from loafing at AB's? The practice was accomplished almost to the point of ceremony.

There was of course much more going on in the village where I grew up than I realized at the time. Those years passed slowly for me. But then, going downhill is usually quicker than going up. At The Shop, the unspoken goal of each loafer was to decrease entropy by turning back the clock. Theirs are true stories well told which, according to authorities on the genre, defines creative non-fiction. None of those principal actors was a lazy storyteller. Thanks to them, the past survives in the sense of human attachment to place, the depth of connections, and the collective memory of many incidents, some intimately linked to events on the world stage.

In case you haven't noticed, the past is still happening. It's been repeating itself in plain view, much like the recycling of seasons through time. To paraphrase William Faulkner, the past isn't dead, and it certainly isn't even past. But Shakespeare said it best, for in the present context, "What's past is prologue." The task of narrator here translates to pouring old wine into new bottles.

December Disaster (1917)

Arthur Benjamin Lohnes, the chief cook at Imperial Oil's Imperoyal Refinery project in Woodside, Dartmouth, watches in disbelief in the bright early Thursday morning of December 6, 1917, as the spacious building trembles and a waiter drops a large pile of breakfast dishes on the dining room floor.

"What's going on, Cook?" the lad exclaims. "There's no blasting scheduled for this morning, is there?"

Equally bewildered, Arthur stands by while the waiter cleans up the mess. He does his best to calm the kitchen staff, but they've already headed outside to check out the situation.

What they see, several miles to the southwest, is a huge yellowish-grey tower of smoke rising steadily into the upper atmosphere.

"Where's that at?" asks one of the workers as he picks himself up off the ground, burdened only a moment before by a heavy box of carpenter's tools.

"Must be at the docks," replies a companion, helping his buddy gather up the tools. "Quite an explosion, I'd say."

"Well, it's not the ammunition magazine, or we'd be in serious trouble," says another.

"Looks like trouble enough, if you ask me. Looks like the bloody Germans are here right enough."

By this time a small crowd has gathered along the rutted track by the large building which, in parallel with several others, occupies part of the thousand-acre plot destined to accommodate the Imperoyal Refinery.

The whole place is soon abuzz with rumours of a German attack on Halifax harbour facilities, or a coordinated U-Boat attack on shipping in the outer harbour. Later that morning, however, the general truth of the matter emerges when plant superintendent William B. Elsworth pays a visit to the construction camp's dining room.

As Elsworth meets with Arthur in the dining hall he does not mince words. "There's been a huge explosion in the Narrows. A munitions ship exploded after colliding with a steamer. There's been fearsome damage to life and property, so our company will do its utmost to contribute to the recovery effort. We're well-equipped to do so. Details are being worked out. I'll keep you informed as best I can.

"But you have to appreciate that extra work will be required of all of you in the days ahead. I expect construction of the refinery to be put on hold while our crews focus on work in Halifax and Dartmouth. There are thousands of homeless families. Those people need to be housed and fed, and generally speaking, cared for. I believe we are well-positioned to help out on this."

By late afternoon, radio reports reveal the scale of the disaster. To make matters worse, there is a rapid change in weather conditions. Already a light snowfall heralds the development of a winter storm. After dinner that evening, Elsworth meets again with Arthur.

"It's bad, Arthur. The war has come to us. But I have to say, thank God for the army. Their medical corps and hospital facilities are crucial to the recovery effort. Several relief trains of the Intercolonial Railway have already arrived in Halifax with medics and supplies."

"So how can we help?" Arthur asks.

"Head office has worked quickly on this. The company is

The main dining hall at the Imperial Oil construction site, Woodside, Dartmouth, December, 1917. Arthur stands in the aisle with a hat and no tie, while William Elsworth is in a vest.

donating ten thousand dollars to the Dartmouth Relief Committee and they've advised us to ready three bunkhouses. These should be adequate to accommodate about two hundred people. We must see to it that competent caretakers are on hand to welcome them. All available construction material and our entire labour force are being rushed to the cities to build shelters. Conditions are even worse than we feared. Word is there's thousands of dead and as many or more homeless and injured. We'll be taking in some of the refugees here, so we'd better plan on doubling up. They will need to be fed. This is where you come in."

"We'll do our best, William."

And so it was in the days following. The company proved itself as good as Elsworth's word. Work on the refinery, although only three months short of completion, was put on hold. From its 3,500 feet of marine frontage on the shore east of George's Island, Imperial Oil's dock allowed boats easy access to the devastated areas of both Halifax and Dartmouth.

Immediately following the explosion, work crews with supplies and tools made their way to severely damaged sites to repair homes and build temporary shelters. Survivors, including several from the devastated Mi'kmaq village at Turtle Grove, were in dire need of help. Among the traumatized were fifty to sixty children. Relief efforts call for team work. Imperoyal's efforts mirrored the efficient work swiftly begun by other civil authorities in the disaster zones on either side of the harbour, by the military and by volunteer organizations – a truly remarkable response carried out in the face of daunting odds.

Amidst the screaming nightmare, the plight of children was naturally the focus of particular concern. As a measure of the efficiency of the rescue effort, most of the people taken in by Imperial Oil workers already bore bandages in one place or another – heads, arms, and hands. It was but one of many scenes not easily forgotten.

Christmas came and went quickly, but not before Arthur helped to organize a collection from the workers to provide gifts for the children. All things considered, not a particularly big deal, Arthur thinks to himself, but still an important contribution to help ease, in whatever way, a human tragedy.

Early in the New Year, Imperoyal's construction workers resumed work on the refinery. Commissioning took place on February 10, 1918, one year after the completion of the trans-shipment plant. Of the Halifax Explosion episode in the company's history, Elsworth understated the case for everyone in the company magazine, *Imperial Oil Review*: "One incident occurred during the construction that will not be forgotten while the memory of the war lasts."

Arthur's wife, Carrie, likely never forgot it either. Following the explosion on December 6, 1917, Carrie did not hear from her husband for ten long days. It was, therefore, with great relief, after the dust settled and the roads were cleared of snow and ferry service restored across Halifax harbour, that Arthur was able to make his way home to Rose Bay and the warmest of welcomes.

Community Life

Arthur Benjamin Lohnes, the second oldest of eight sons and two daughters of Edward Rufus Lohnes and Elmina Catherine Backman, was born on January 28, 1887, on Second Peninsula and baptized in the Lutheran Church. The family moved to a small farm in Upper Rose Bay when Arthur was a young boy. Charles, the first born, died in infancy. Arthur shouldered a great deal of responsibility for the family farm and younger siblings. Through it all, he managed to attend school to the seventh grade.

Shortly after his twentieth birthday, Arthur sailed as a cook on a salt banker. He tried this experiment twice, but his susceptibility to seasickness ruled out this career. With him he took a seven-hundred-page tome on the fine art of cooking. Published in the year of his birth, *The White House Cook Book* has the intriguing subtitle *Cooking, toilet and household recipes, menus, dinner-giving, table etiquette, care of the sick, health suggestions, facts*. His copy is annotated: "A.B. Lohnes, Rose Bay, N.S. March 15, 1910 and Dec. 22, 1911. Arrived home Dec. 20 had to keep the house for a week. Not much snow before Christmas." Its origin has been a family puzzle for over a hundred years. The cookbook is a compendium of interesting recipes ranging from plain to exotic. One has to doubt it proved much help to AB while at sea, particularly as it survived largely unblemished. No one can say how AB came to possess it – not even his youngest daughter, Margaret Jean.

Upon gaining dry land, AB abandoned his oars and promptly headed into the woods. His mind was made up. His courtship with Carrie Lenora Wentzell, a young lady from Riverport, advanced to a formal engagement in September 1911.

Engagement photograph of Arthur Benjamin Lohnes and Carrie Lenora Wentzell, September 1913.

They married on December 17, 1913, and lived in AB's parents' home while their own was under construction across the road from the Lohnes homestead. Most of the wood for his house came from his family's woodlot at nearby Atlantic Seaside. AB took part in all aspects of the construction project – from logging and milling the wood, to the various phases of house building.

To help make ends meet, Arthur served as a cook for the Davison Lumber Company in logging camps near Gold River, Lunenburg County. At the turn of the century, logging employed thousands of men in Nova Scotia. By far the largest part of this very big business was run by Davison out of Bridgewater. For the better part of two years, AB and Carrie were responsible for feeding fifty or more men in various logging camps. *White House Cook Book* or not, it could not have been a trivial assignment.

By 1916, confident in his ability to cook on a large scale, AB applied to Imperial Oil Company for employment at the construction site of a new trans-shipment oil facility at Woodside in Dartmouth. AB and his wife were happy when he landed the job. Both agreed it would be nice to return to civilization. Pay might be only marginally better than in the logging business, but there were bound to be perks. He was advised he would need to plan on an 84-hour work week, six 12-hour days, and a 12-hour Sunday shift every other week – the norm for Imperial Oil employees. That would not leave much time for family life. In 1917, when conscription came into effect, Arthur was considered exempt because of his participation in essential war work.

Imperoyal was intended to serve as a trans-shipment facility for Mexican crude oil from steam tanker ships to rail cars, for delivery to the Montreal refinery. However, shortly after AB's arrival the decision was made to build a refinery instead. The Dartmouth refinery would be just one of several being built across Canada as World War I ramped up. The location was originally the site of Fort Clarence, an eighteenth-century bastion guarding the harbour against attack. When construction finished, AB returned to Rose Bay. Their first daughter, Estelle, was born on September 17, 1918. Margaret Jean arrived twelve years later on May 18, 1930.

A 1938 family portrait shows Arthur Benjamin Lohnes, wife Carrie Lenora, and daughters Margaret Jean and Estelle Caroline. .

* * * * *

For those growing up in Upper Rose Bay in the middle of the last century, access to AB's store was considered a birthright by the younger generation. Though first and foremost a general store – Groceries, Fruit and Meats, as the sign on AB's calendar proclaimed – it was also a significant meeting place, a church of sorts, with regular communicants. In lockstep with the seasons, residents worked according to various rituals: planting in spring, berry-picking and picnicking in summer, fishing in all seasons except during the depths of winter, gathering harvest and fuel in the fall, and surviving in winter.

The social history of the community embodied the very spirit of the place, and nothing exemplified this better than when loafers gathered to exchange news and views at AB's. Occasionally a woman might be present to make a purchase, or young boys, but the evening gatherings around AB's beautiful pot-bellied stove were mostly men, first to come, and last to leave. Year-round, but especially in fall and winter, memorable yarns were spun, in a language distinctly foreign in pronunciation, terms, and syntax. For the loafers, the occasion served as a release from their acquired bondage to the sea – all in the patriarchal tradition of the county's Foreign Protestant settlers who arrived from Europe more than two centuries earlier.

The Shop, as it was known to members of his family (and as referred to in this book), was a remarkably unpretentious structure, though it endured as a general store for nearly forty years. The origin of the building is uncertain. AB opened it initially as an ice cream parlour. His chief competitor in this field was Gabriel Zinck's shop on the Riverport waterfront, which also boasted a locally famous barber shop. Before long, The Shop morphed into a regular country store despite stiff competition from others in the district.

As a general store, The Shop's main competitor was Ritcey Brothers Ltd. in Riverport. The Ritceys have played key roles in the life and commerce of the community as far back as 1852, when Thomas Ritcey opened the first store in Riverport. They would become a dominant force in the local business culture, weaving most of the general stores into their commercial chain. Not to be outdone, a merchant named Oxner opened for business in the "Oxner Big House," an impressive four-storey edifice near Oxners Beach. This house was basically an inn, a multi-faceted business, renowned in its time for offering many bedrooms, several apartments, two dance floors, a bar, and a well-stocked wine cellar. The building was demolished in 1936.

Samuel Ritcey established a second large general store in 1892, on the shore opposite the site later occupied by Ritcey Brothers Ltd. Following the disastrous Riverport waterfront fire in 1920, Samuel retired, and his son Russell teamed up with Robie Creaser to rebuild. Their enterprise, Ritcey and Creaser

Ltd., included a wharf, carried a wider selection of goods than Ritcey Brothers, and was heavily patronized by serious shoppers and loafers alike.

Adelaide Seaboyer MacGregor from Rose Bay – whose Scottish husband, Dr. Murdock MacGregor, settled in Riverport in 1871 and established a medical practice – opened a small store in 1879. It was later taken over by their son, Hector. Hector's enterprising spirit led him, at age eighteen, to initiate the weekly *Riverport Times* in 1904. With a circulation of about four hundred, the paper ceased publication after about a year. Hector opened a second general store in Feltzen South, which he sold to Charles Zellers in 1913.

MacGregor's Riverport store grew into the extensive business of Ritcey Brothers Ltd. after being bought out in 1915 by Charles H. and St. Clair Ritcey. They easily persuaded Zellers to operate his Feltzen South store as a branch of Ritcey Brothers. After the brothers set up their store as a ship-outfitting and general merchandise firm, Charles and his wife and family moved into the store and occupied the upper storey. St. Clair left the company in 1930 due to illness, and passed away in 1931 at the age of thirty-nine.

Prior to their move above the store, Charles and his wife Amy Himmelman lived next door to the present location of the Myrtle Hotel. Their home was a miner's cottage, one of several floated into Riverport and District after the gold rush at the Ovens ended in the mid-1860s. It's hard to conceive now, but in the 1860s the Ovens mining camp was a bustling community of over six hundred people.

For the record, Captain Stephen (Stevie) Oxner and his wife Anna Ritcey began construction of the Myrtle Hotel in 1900 and completed it in 1902. Named for their daughter Myrtle Jean, the hotel was a prominent enterprise, complete with livery stable, conveniently located on the shore front. The Myrtle Hotel was home also to the Riverport Board of Trade, founded in 1908 in which Dr. W.H. MacDonald served as president, Daniel H. Romkey as vice president, and Samuel

Ritcey as secretary. Myrtle Jean, who married William Romkey, inherited the building and though the name Myrtle sticks to the building, she always insisted on being called Jean or Jeannie. Jeannie's son, Lorne, somehow acquired the nickname Al Capone. Over the years, this name too has stuck to the place. Rumour endures that the notorious Chicago gangster – the real Al – stayed at the Myrtle Hotel during Prohibition. Those rumours are false.

In AB's day, country general stores proliferated – many are listed by Jean Mosher in *Home Town Recipes of Riverport and District*. In Lower Rose Bay, a popular general store (started by John and Forman Risser) was run by Sam Risser and his son Bernard. This store and its owners play an important part in *Rum Tales*.

Martin Wentzell's shoe store was situated on the "Cosy Corner" at the south end of the bridge across Ritceys Cove in Riverport. A stone's throw distant was Pat Wentzell's bicycle shop, and across the street from that, Arthur Conrad's cobbler's shop. Martin's store replaced a combined hat shop and ice cream parlour. Some oldsters, who as children were outfitted there with church-worthy shoes, recall the thrill of watching their toes wiggle under his X-ray machine, the cutting edge of wild innovation said to help ensure a perfect fit. The use of this device across the nation occurred about the same time cheap wrist watches with luminous dials made their debut. Those watches provided sparkling entertainment for many little boys and girls in their beds after dark. The luminescence was caused by radium, a highly radioactive element painted on the dials. The craze for these watches lasted well after Hiroshima.

Wholesale grocers supplying many of these stores included Rafuse & Eisenhauer Ltd. of Bridgewater and the Halifax firm H.Y. Payzant, for hardware items. LaHave Creamery supplied dairy products. AB used their butterboxes to contain various hardware items such as nails, nuts, and bolts. Unfortunately, the operators of the Ideal Maternity Home in Chester used their LaHave Creamery boxes as coffins to dispose of the "butterbox babies" who died while in their care from 1926 to 1946.

The general store run by Charles Zellers in Feltzen South was one of the better known. Perhaps Zellers, like his friend AB, suffered incurably from *mal de mer*, for he too began work as a sea cook. Both men experienced close-up the Halifax Explosion. At the time, Charles and his wife were staying on Argyle Street while in the city buying supplies for Christmas. Zellers' store played an important part in the community's social network for over fifty years until destroyed by fire on March 30, 1970. It carried a range of goods from groceries and clothing to coal oil and cattle feed. The last two items were delivered from Halifax to Riverport by coastal vessels whereas various other goods were retailed at scattered country outposts by "travellers" or "dealers," i.e. travelling salesmen.

Ritcey Brothers Ltd. also owned the store at the Crossroads in Rose Bay, and for many years ran it as a branch store. The story of the Crossroads store feeds into that of AB's. Originally the brainchild of sea captain Rufus Himmelman, it faced a start as challenging as that faced by AB's small enterprise.

* * * * *

The store at the Crossroads began in the home built by Captain Rufus Himmelman and his wife Jediah in 1893. That same year the telephone line was put through the district. Three battery-operated phones were installed – one at Samuel Ritcey's store in Riverport, one at the post office in Rose Bay, and one at Rissers' general store in Lower Rose Bay. Electric lighting arrived in 1914.

In 1895, Captain Rufus began a small store on the east side of his home. Unfortunately, due to pneumonia contracted during the rigours of winter weather on the Grand Banks, he passed away in 1897 at the age of thirty-seven. After his death, store and house were connected, enabling his wife Jediah to continue to support her family.

Among the old Foreign Protestants, the name Himmelman – man of Heaven – derives from far nobler roots than, for example, Mossman, which was issued in the ancient days of Swiss serfdom for "labourers who worked for Moss." G. Lawrence Himmelman, son of Captain Rufus and Jediah, lived up to the family name.

At eighteen, Lawrence left the village to study for the ministry at Thiel College, Pennsylvania, an institution founded by early German Lutheran immigrant investors. He followed up this ecclesiastical education with a stint at Chicago Theological Seminary in Maywood, Illinois. He worked hard, and left an impressive legacy. All three of his sons – Paul, Donald, and Robert – followed his lead, becoming ministers in the Lutheran Church. Unlike numerous other famous Himmelmans who forged their fame as blue water captains, Lawrence and his sons turned their backs on the sea. Captain Rufus doubtless might have been impressed, though unlikely to admit to there being more Himmelman ministers than Himmelman sea captains in Riverport and District.

Jediah's store at the Crossroads has enjoyed a checkered history through several different operators, most of them under the direction of Ritcey Brothers Ltd. Like many other general stores in Riverport and District, the genealogy of the Crossroads store reads like a biblical account of begats. It has most recently experienced an exciting rebirth as the Rose Bay General Store, owned and operated by industrious modern foreign Protestant Germans, Anja and Christoph Henschel.

* * * * *

AB enjoyed working at The Shop. He always dreamed of being his own boss, a human condition commonly confused with independence. He was able to make a living while close to family. He was happy to be able to help sustain the economy and to contribute to the area's social life. Such was the reality of many such small country general stores. Today, sparks of social interaction via episodic TV "corner store" revelations continue to catch and hold the public's eye.

For several years, AB operated a gas pump in front of The Shop for the convenience of the motoring public. Close to the south side of The Shop, he kept an ice house and a coal shed. In the early days, a warehouse was located between these buildings and the school (a short distance further south), and served as a meeting hall for the Masons. Their gatherings were conducted by AB dressed in high order Independent Order of Odd Fellows regalia. Normally he kept his tall black hat and special apron out of sight in a spare bedroom at home. A good man of high principles, honest, modest, fussy, and hard-working, he could just as well have been a preacher except he was not given to preaching – unless that occurred during Masons' meetings.

In stocking The Shop, AB likely took a good deal of advice from Charles Zellers. Merchandise offered by The Shop differed only in minor detail from that offered in the Feltzen South store. The Shop stocked no ladies undergarments, girdles, and other unmentionables. Nor, so far as I am aware, did any of the regular patrons store a personal gallon jar of rum in The Shop for their convenience and that of friends who preferred not to drink at home. But this was a long-established custom in Zellers' store, where it fully met with the operator's approval. "They didn't want to take it home because that way, they'd drink it that much faster," said Charles. AB did his best to make it known he didn't approve of the practice carried out in Zellers' store, much as he might otherwise have admired his fellow entrepreneur. His were strong principles of right and wrong.

AB and his family might have been viewed by neighbours as being well off, even affluent, but the fact is, no one got rich running a country general store. The long arm of commerce represented by Ritcey Brothers Ltd. didn't facilitate things for AB. AB was frugal. Signs of this lasting trait became conspicuous to observers over time. One example is the way he conserved gas on his way to work. Wind and weather permitting, after starting off at speed from his hilltop home, he turned off the engine of his car and coasted the entire distance of slightly over one kilometre to The Shop. Harry Conrad, a local authority on mechanical propulsion, reportedly tried it on the dirt road of the day and confirmed that it could be done.

If AB was accused of parsimony, there were good reasons for it. The Shop faced stiff competition, especially during its start-up years. Thanks to that mysterious sub-contract to Ritcey Brothers Ltd., the Crossroads store had a rather easier commercial time of it. Unable to offer purchases on credit, however, the Crossroads store was perceived by some people as the less user-friendly option.

AB was constantly challenged to keep the opposition in sight, even though each and every day on his way to and from work he passed by in front of it. There it stood, scarcely more than a slingshot's distance from The Shop. Clara Meisner, the younger of two spinster sisters, tended the Crossroads store for many decades; her stay-at-home sister, Mary, kept turkeys and in her spare time hooked elaborate rugs.

The Crossroads store, focusing as it did on dry goods, never really caught on in popularity the way AB's did. The store lacked the cheese and variety of groceries of AB's. Clara never seemed the least bit thrilled to find little boys in her store looking around for penny candy. Worse yet, from their jaundiced point of view, she didn't stock fish hooks. Nobody, not even grown-ups, loafed at the Crossroads store. It could only have happened if you had to wait in line – which wasn't very often, as I recall. Plus, there was no pot-bellied stove, and even worse, no chairs, and there's not a lot of fun loafing while standing up.

Pleasing the customer was not always an easy matter for AB. When vessels returned after months of work on the

Grand Banks, many of the discharged sailors made promptly to a place that supplied the "good stuff" – liquor. Rolling
home, they likely enjoyed a good meal prepared by "the mis-
sus" from purchases made at AB's store and "put on their bill."
Some of the seamen had very poor memories, and once they
had returned to sea, their family was hungry again. What does
a poor soft-hearted grocer do? Carrie might have urged Arthur
to be more assertive, but this was not in his nature. People
knew him as basically good-natured, and in truth, his respect
for others vied strongly with his patience and tolerance when
problems in business dealings arose.

* * * * *

After AB opened his store circa 1919, a small body of
loafers began to show up regularly, especially on Saturday
evenings when The Shop usually remained open late. Otherwise, his was a nine to six operation (with time out for a quick
lunch), unless by special request he agreed to remain open on a
weekday evening. This was mostly dependent on which ships
and how many were in port. Among the seamen, a few were
young enough to have been conscripted or recruited during the
war, but as fishermen were considered essential to the war effort, they had been exempt from military service.

News of social events made the rounds quickly despite
sparse telephone service. Dial service did not begin until 1938.
Prior to this, the several homes which invested in the device
were served by "party lines." As several houses shared the
same telephone line, each customer had their own specific
ring, but neighbours could pick up their own phone and listen in to anyone's conversation. Thus, "breaking news" got
around quickly. The one long and two short to AB's home was
one of the rings most frequently heard after hours, more often
than not from party-goers seeking cigarettes and soft drinks
for mixers. AB never took the trouble to have a phone installed

in The Shop; however, the camaraderie enjoyed by loafers often short-circuited the phone service.

For the record, two large (quart-sized) dry cell batteries housed in wooden boxes were used in each battery-operated telephone. When the batteries eventually lost their power, the telephone company would come and change them. Usually the company asked if the homeowner wished to keep them for use as fuel in their furnace in order to clean out the creosote from the chimneys. Dry cell batteries of the day ranged widely in compositions, though the chemistry of those used in Riverport and District is not known with certainty. The main ingredient (matrix) in any case will have been carbon. Reportedly their burning created an intense heat which accomplished the job of chimney cleaning in short order.

* * * * *

Now picture AB in apron strings, mid-day in early October 1919, busy unpacking and sorting out merchandise prior to shelving on his first day of business. Turning, he notices a tall man who enters after a brief rap at the door.

"Hey there, Arthur, how are you makin' out?"

"Laurie Mossman! Welcome home! We half expected never to see you again! Home safe – thank goodness, returned in one piece for a wonder!"

The two men shake hands and then stand back, as if to assess any differences in each other since their last meeting.

"I heard you'd come ashore for good, but never expected to find you here," Laurie says, more a question than a statement of fact, as he warms his hands in front of AB's pot-bellied stove. A rather fancy model, it has mica glass windows in front and blue enamelled trim.

"Yes," answers AB, "my stomach left me no choice in the matter. I'd ha' been better off joining up to go overseas with you fellows in the 85th."

"Aw, don't feel bad. You didn't miss much," Laurie says, absentmindedly admiring the stove and soaking up the radiated warmth, as it winks and glows its way through the day. A head taller than AB, he is momentarily at a loss for words, thinking to himself that no one who wasn't there, on the Western Front, could ever hope to understand. That's just the way it was.

"So, how about you, Laurie … what are your plans?"

"Well … I've got to find something. I've bought a house over at 121 North Side Road, in Riverport," he adds proudly. "Paid for most of the six hundred dollars it cost me out of my regimental payout for time served, but I still have to find two hundred or so to get the creditors off my back. Might as well try fishin' out of Riverport for a while. I hear they've been doing pretty well lately. And Blanche, she wants to get married."

"I hear they just launched a new schooner in Lunenburg, the *General Haig*. There could be an opening or two on board her if you're interested."

"I plan to look around a bit. But I'd get myself a rowboat before I sign onto anything that carries that name. We had enough of him overseas."

AB wisely decides not to pursue the topic further. Despite censorship, serious mutterings of discontent concerning the leadership of the British Expeditionary Force (BEF) on the Western Front had seeped through to some of Britain's most distant allies. The terms "mutual attrition" and "wastage" were just a couple of the criticisms levelled against Haig's command. Changing the subject, he says, "You and Blanche were seeing each other even before the war, weren't you?"

"No, I was back for a while before we got together. But I'm not havin' much help from what's his name next door – you know, her father, Captain Himmelman. He can't seem to stand the sight of me … never could. Must be I remind him of somethin' he'd rather forget. And the worst of it is, I don't know what I ever done to get him so riled up."

"Oh … Bertie … well, he can be pretty grouchy at times.

Since his wife passed away, Frances Gaudley looks after the place for him. Her husband Kenneth died a long while back, leaving her with three children. Two of their girls, Louise and Carrie, stay in that neat little cottage out near the road ... but I don't know about the other. Could be Old Bertie's sea sick – he's been a long time at sea."

"Couldn't ha' been that long a stretch. He's got about a dozen children. You'd think the man would be more understanding."

"I don't know about that ..."

"Mornin'," says the young woman who enters The Shop just then. "I'm not interruptin', am I?"

"Hardly, Mrs Zinck," Arthur hastens to reply. "Welcome! You are one of my first customers. Just opened for business ... very first time today," he adds proudly. "Thursa, you remember Laurie, don't you, from down Riverport way? He's a cousin of Titus. They're both back from overseas. They were with the Nova Scotia Highlanders. Laurie, this is Thursa, Frank Zinck's wife. They live across the road, in the brown house on the corner."

"Overseas, oh my Lord! Thank Heavens that's over with. Welcome home, Laurie. What you men must ha' gone through."

"Thanks, it's good to be back, I can tell you," says Laurie, in classic understatement.

"I heard they had a party for you fellows out in Upper Kingsburg ... at Titus's home, I believe," says Thursa.

"Yes," AB confirms, "only right too," musing that there would have been a few faces absent at that get-together. Not least among the missing would have been Laurie's brother, Marshall.

Thursa edges her way toward the huge wheel of cheese which Arthur has set out beside the counter. "Umm! Arthur, won't you cut me a nice junk of this cheese? Frank's just back from the Banks. He loves rat trap cheese. He'll be some pleased. This will be a real treat for him. He'll be down to visit before long, I'll be bound."

"No problem, Mrs. Zinck. Here, I'll slice some off for you."

"It's real nice havin' a store handy like this, next door. Did you know there was a store in our house before Frank and I moved in? Henry Wentzell ran it as a dry goods store. And a fur salesman comes 'round every once in a while to visit. He had a wonderful supply of furs, but only the rich could afford them."

"No, I didn't know that," AB responds. "I don't think I'll be getting into that line of business for a while."

"And I'll need some pork chops. Oh, I see you got raisin bread too. Here, I've made a list. How 'bouts I just give you my list. Put it all on my account please, if you don't mind," she goes on.

AB forces a somewhat lopsided grin and bears the unstated threat of possible nonpayment, the first of many such encounters he'd be left to deal with along his path of private enterprise. During the next few minutes, he's occupied putting together Thursa's grocery order. Then he hastily musters a wave and a hearty "Come again, Laurie!" just as the ex-soldier eases himself out of The Shop. Laurie has completely forgotten to obtain the box of snuff he meant to purchase.

Before very long news gets around that AB's store is up and running. Within a week or two it becomes part of the local landscape, a convenience that for all anyone knows might go on forever. Competing for attention with the pot-bellied stove, AB's cheese wheel proves enormously popular. An odd competing centrepiece of attraction, it is positioned in a glass-fronted cabinet on top of the cash register. On the right-hand side of it is a glassed-in case of penny candy: honeymoons, maple buds, chicken legs, Turkish delight, coconut balls, and caramel suckers that resembled bats – all sorts of interesting things. Exciting drinks are on offer too – Kik, as either bright tasty orange or cola, and cream soda, a sweet abiding attraction for young tongues that know no better.

There's no doubt the opening of The Shop resulted in sharpened competition for the numerous items considered

Alexander Layng's painting shows The Shop, shed, and gas pump beside Arthurs Brook (at right); the road to Rose Bay and Kingsburg fronts the store. Artistic license includes a single clove placed by the artist on the left-hand side of the painting, in memory of a fire in late 1957 which resulted in closure of The Shop. (The bottle of cloves, unaffected by the extensive smoke damage, is kept in the Lohnes family to this day.)

essential for running the average household. AB kept only enough coal to supply his pot-bellied stove. But The Shop carried fuel oil (kerosene) and gasoline, in addition to the numerous variations on the theme advertised on AB's annual calendar: *ARTHUR B. LOHNES, Groceries, Fruit and Meats, Rose Bay, Nova Scotia*. Bolded letters beneath the months declared: *For Pastry and Cakes Robin Hood Flour, Milled from Washed Wheat*. As proclaimed on a sign on the huge shed next to The Shop, he sold ice too. That essential was laboriously sawn and hauled in winter from Gocky's Lake below Arthur's house, then thoroughly packed in sawdust. AB was a busy man.

Julian Byng's Promotion (August 14, 1923)

"I've sailed wit' him, an' he's a decent captain, damn good fisherman too. A year or so back, he was the high-liner, the guy who caught the most fish," says Roy Deal. He and Titus Mossman are the first to arrive that evening. The discussion in progress is sparked by their protests over Laurie Mossman's comments concerning Captain Haliburton (Bertie) Himmelman, Laurie's possible future father-in-law.

"Well, you don't know him as well as I do," insists Laurie. "He hates the sight of me. We're just lucky he's not here this evening. He can make things downright unpleasant. If I can ever get the money together, me and Blanche might have to elope. Bertie would never get over the insult, but what else can we do?"

"Bertie can be pretty ornery once his mind's made up on something or other. He'll maybe come 'round in time," AB offers from behind the counter.

"I hope so. It's kind of hard on his wife too, let alone Blanche."

"What's this I hear, you've decided not to go fishing?" says AB, changing the subject.

"Well, I tried it one trip, but the asthma acted up so bad."

"That's likely a holdover from you being gassed," Titus muses.

"Yes," Laurie admits. "You should know. You was one of them as discovered me late that day."

"That was just a few days before the Armistice, I remember. The Hun was lobbing over gas artillery shells that morning. You got a pretty good blighty too, the wound that got you back to England, I remember."

"Yeah, got me in the upper leg. Laid me out there for quite a while. Don't remember a whole lot about it … rather not."

"We understand," says Roy, "them things are best forgotten."

Happy to take his cue from Roy, Laurie says, "I been meanin' to tell you, Arthur, I got me a job ashore as a traveller for Ritcey Brothers. I'm not gonna be able to help you. I'd like to, but I'm not allowed. I'm workin' for them now … deliverin' supplies to the Crossroads store and a couple of others. Ritcey Brothers looks after its own. They call the shots. I guess you know how it is. Sorry."

"Can't do much about that," says AB. "A man's got to do what he got to do. Still, nothing says you can't come by and see us when you can manage. You're always welcome. So far, for grocery supplies, I've been dealing with Rafuse and Eisenhauer up in Bridgewater, and that's working out pretty well. They're right beside the railway station. LaHave Creamery is across the road from them, and they keep me well supplied with ice cream and butter – about the best there is. You may have seen Freddie Allen come by here with their yellow truck. I keep ice stored in the ice house beside The Shop. As needed, I bring some into the back room and put it in an ice chest."

"Looks like you're set up pretty good here, well organized," says Laurie. "Where do you get your ice?"

"A couple of young fellas helped cut it out with me at the pond below Gocky's – Obediah Wentzell's – place just down the hill from my house."

"Oh, and is he still blacksmithin'?"

"Yes, he is. He's right handy at that. Gets all the business he can handle. By the way, how'd you boys make out rubbin' shoulders with Baron Byng and his good lady in Bridgewater last Tuesday?" AB asks.

"Baron Byng, and what all else ... Knight of this and Lord of that ... why, the man has more titles than scales on a kyack," says Roy.

"He's earned them all, if you really want to know," says Titus, quick to defend the Canadian Corp's champion at Vimy Ridge. "Pity he's gone and joined up with the wrong crowd. That Mackenzie King's an odd bird. He's got some strange ways."

"He can't help that, Titus," says Roy. "He was probably born that way. Anyways, someone or other probably appointed Byng to be Governor General."

"Now who could that have been?" Titus asks, not really expecting an answer.

"Mackenzie King?" offers Austin. "Who else would it be?"

"It was in the paper just a few days ago," says AB, who, last thing every evening, sits down with the newspaper to soak up the news of the day. "Somebody named Churchill, Winston Churchill. Ever hear of him? Secretary of State for the Colonies, I believe it read."

"You don't miss much. But time will tell. King's got some mighty peculiar ways, even for a Liberal," Titus mutters, though he does not elaborate

"We'll see if he and King get along." AB concludes. "He's lasted two years already. I expect Byng's his own man. He'll not be pushed around by anyone, not even by Mackenzie King. But remember, King won the election last year on the slimmest of margins. I doubt he'll be able to hang on very long – at least some of us hope not. So what was it like last Tuesday, up in Bridgewater?"

"Me and Laurie went up to the civic reception. A lot of the Byng Boys showed up. We all have a lot of respect for General Byng," says Titus, adding, "He was our CO at Vimy."

"Veterans were invited to attend and meet General Byng. Titus and I went overseas on the *Olympic* together in October 1916," explains Laurie. "We trained for months at Witley Military Camp in southern England. My brother went over on the same ship a couple of months earlier than us … in July."

"It was while you was at Witley they transferred you to the 85th, wasn't it?" asks Titus.

"Yes, I started out in the 219th Regiment. Then it was disbanded, leaving only the 85th Highlanders intact as a Nova Scotia regiment. On February 10, '17, we crossed the channel to France from Folkestone. I'll never forget that day."

"Why's that?" asks AB, his curiosity peaked by the talk of these two recently demobbed soldiers.

"Step short! Step short!" Laurie laughs, "Titus, do you remember that sergeant yelling that warning as we marched down the steps to the quay in Folkestone to board the S.S. *London*? It was a fairly steep ramp, and a couple of fellows either didn't hear or didn't understand. They tripped up and set off a domino effect on about a dozen others ahead of them. The sergeant major just about went crazy."

"They were lucky they didn't get sent down to 'Eat Apples' (Étaples) for more training," Titus remarks, tongue in cheek. He is a veteran who learned first-hand about how that particular British Expeditionary Force depot and transit camp functioned.

"Bridgewater?" someone repeats AB's earlier question.

"Yes, Bridgewater. Well," says Titus, "there was a huge turnout … hundreds, maybe a thousand or more, I heard tell, and as many again in Lunenburg on the day after. At Bridgewater a lot of us showed up, dressed up all proper, like on parade. The Boy Scouts and Girl Guides were lined up there too, at the platform when the train came in, all spit and polish. Commander Byng and his wife and all their friends and attendants travel in style. He took his time in Bridgewater. He shook hands with all of us, and had a word or two with every man. He's a soldier's soldier."

"Then we was all marched down to the high school auditorium for the speech-makin'," Laurie adds. "The mayor of Bridgewater … what's his name …?

"Marshall," Willy Kaizer tells him.

'Yes, Marshall," said Laurie, hesitating as he says the name, "and he gave a long speech congratulating Byng on his promotion to Governor General. For his part the Commander kept his speech short – couldn't ha' been more than ten minutes long."

"He's got his work cut out for him, dealing with them Liberals," says Titus, ever the staunch Conservative. "And there was Billy Ernst, from Mahone Bay, Captain William Ernst, I should say, gave the address to Commander Byng on behalf of the veterans. A mighty fine man is Captain Ernst. He was with us at Vimy … and Bourlon Wood too, come to think of it, right through to the end."

"But Byng was the real hero at Vimy, wasn't he?" asks AB.

"That's true enough," says Titus. "He's a professional soldier, not a stuffed shirt like most of the British brass. We liked him well – still do. At Vimy, we was proud to be known as the Byng Boys. He and General Currie worked well together on most things, but both of 'em was strong-willed. Currie generally had the last word. Raids was one thing they definitely did not agree on, I remember that. The CO, he figured the more men on a raid, the better the chances of getting prisoners. Currie, he reckoned we were best off using only two or three men to get a prisoner for information. You see, all was needed was the ID of the particular unit they was with. All that stuff that is stitched on their uniforms. 'Course, if you could get 'em to talk, that was a bonus. But like I said, in the end, after a few disastrous big raids, Currie ended up havin' the last word. He only became commander of the Canadian Corps after Haig ordered Byng to join Allenby's Third Army."

"After the stopover in Lunenburg, Governor Byng, accompanied by William Duff, our Member of Parliament, also made a trip by car down to Riverport," says Laurie.

"I went to the affair in Riverport," says AB. "Both made short speeches in front of the Bank of Montreal. There was a surprising big turnout. A lot like a garden party, except for the speech-makin' of course."

"What did the Governor General say to you at the station in Bridgewater?" AB asks Titus.

"Oh, nothing much, just 'How are you,' that sort of thing. He never said anything to me over there either. At Vimy I was only a Lance Corporal. But like Currie, Byng made a point of knowing all the senior NCOs by name. But I remember him, going over the mock-up of what we had to do, come Zero Hour. We had a big scale model of Vimy Ridge rigged up on the ground behind the lines. We learned some hard lessons at Vimy. He and Currie were drivers when it come down to details. But it paid off in the end."

"My brother and I both missed out on Vimy," says Laurie.

"That would be Harris, Harris Marshall, right?" AB asks.

"Yes, but he mostly went by Marshall. He was a year older than me, joined at twenty-one, three or four months before I did. He signed up with the 112th Overseas Battalion, but ended up in France with the 25th Battalion just in time for the push north of Vimy along the Arras-Lens road ... reported missing on July 5, 1917, somewhere along the Souchez River."

"Souchez River, oh my God ...," Titus mutters under his breath.

"His body was never found."

"There were a good many others too, I imagine," says Roy.

"I missed Vimy," Laurie volunteers. "I was sick when we first came ashore in France."

"Seasick?" exclaims Roy, horrified.

"No, I came down with diphtheria, complicated by skin problems, impetigo, scabies, and whatnot. Whatever was goin' around, I got it."

"That's terrible. What did they do with you when you got sick?"

"It's a long story. But they put me on a train to Étaples ... that's a huge military hospital complex down a ways along the French coast. A real nice place," says Laurie with a knowing wink and a nod to his cousin, Titus, "... General Hospital No. 24. After recovery from diphtheria, they sent me back to England for more training. It was only in October of the following year I was able to rejoin the 85th."

"You arrived just in time for Valenciennes. And it was no picnic, even at that late stage," says Titus.

"Well, I don't know. Perhaps the worst was over by then."

"Not for you, it wasn't," adds Titus, for he had been there.

"No, it wasn't for me," says Laurie, wishing this conversation had never begun, reluctant to break the culture of silence imbued in most veterans.

"Why's that?" asks Willy, keen to learn the end of this tale, no matter the cost to the teller.

"I took a shot in the leg, upper thigh ... about here," he says, indicating the upper part of his right leg. "And that laid me out for a while. That was along the line of the Honnelle River in Belgium in early November, I forget exactly, I think it was the sixth or seventh of the month. To make it worse, the Germans followed up with a gas attack. Anyways, by the end of the day, I was clear of it all and out of it for good."

"Only a few days before the armistice!" says AB.

"So here we are, home again, makin' our way best we can," says Titus, as happy as his cousin to turn from this brief retrospective on an incident born of global insanity.

"Well, at least as a gas victim you'll receive something by way of a pension," AB points out, recalling that his brother Joshua was also a gas victim, and that he received a pension because of it.

"Yes, I suppose I could. But many fellows are far worse off than me. I don't think I'll bother to apply," says Laurie.

"Don't be so foolish! Go ahead and apply for it," urges Titus. "You're entitled to that much, at least."

A Bit of a Breeze (November 1928)

John Henry Leroy (Roy) Deal was born in 1898, four years earlier than his friend and neighbour, Titus Milton Mossman. Roy was a small, muscular, wiry individual and he lived two houses south of our home, on the opposite side of the road. Except for his friendship and respect for his two younger brothers Aubrey and Dennis, my father got along better with Roy than anyone else I knew. Roy and his wife, Letoile, were good neighbours. Their daughter Elaine was one of my favourite childhood companions.

In 1922 Roy married Letoile Zinck from Feltzen South, a village within Riverport and District. She was a cousin of Richard Zinck of that same village, and although Roy and Letoile lived "happily ever after," Richard and his wife Hattie separated, abandoning their four young children as wards of the county.

The community mindsets of Titus and Roy were much alike, mirroring the roles played by blue water seamen, and as heads of their respective households. On water at least, it must be said both men had travelled widely, though neither considered himself a man of the world.

Roy's chronic emphysema, doubtless exacerbated by chain-smoking, excused him from military service. How he survived decades dwelling among his fellow fishermen in the fuggy fo'c's'les of salt bankers is one of life's many mysteries.

Roy missed out on World War I. Not so my father – Titus was a physically unscathed veteran of that cataclysm, who was forever bedevilled by memories of those years of trench warfare. But neither of the two friends ever did more than briefly mention the topic in passing.

After service in the 85th Battalion, Nova Scotia Highlanders, during World War I (as detailed in *Going Over: A Nova Scotian Soldier in World War I*), Titus headed west to try his luck as a farm hand deep in the prairie of southern Saskatchewan. That life, he discovered, was not for him. But it was the monoculture Marquis wheat, which, as much as anything, helped bring on the devastating drought conditions that drove him as well as many real farmers to forsake the plains for greener pastures.

Back in Rose Bay, older and doubtless somewhat wiser, his romance heated up to the degree that his girlfriend, Helen Viola Spindler, invited him to accompany her to New York state where she had secured a high school teaching position. For Titus, this fresh adventure was essentially a job hunt, although the only employment he was able to find was in a laundry. He decided then and there against "becoming a washer woman," and upon his return to Nova Scotia headed to the waterfront and resumed his former occupation as a sea cook. Subsequently, bad luck on a Lunenburg rum-runner, the *Miserinko*, landed him and fellow crew members with lengthy terms in prison, down in New Albany, New York. This ignominious return to New York cured him of rum-running, though his children knew little more than rumour about that chapter in his life.

Long-suffering souls, Titus and Helen delayed for nearly a decade before they married. Titus was perhaps prompted to this irreversible action by his cousin Laurie Mossman, who wed Blanche Himmelman in mid July 1928 – be it noted, in the absence of the bride's father, Captain Bertie Himmelman.

Shortly after their marriage in September 1928, Titus and Helen had a disastrous car accident. Apparently Titus was the designated driver on that occasion. The car was a brand-new Pontiac, won by Mother. All things considered, her achievement proved a lasting sore point in more ways than one. It has to be said that within the family, the adults' feelings – except for unpredictable explosive intervals induced by Father's PTSD – were held close in check.

Home from a fishing trip, Roy and Titus often accompanied each other to a loafing rendezvous at The Shop. Stranded among their shipmates, as on board ship, these two men were outgoing, voluble, companionable, and garrulous to a degree unheard of within their own homes. In the sheltered setting of The Shop, old hands and their buddies were cheered by recounting adventures – in effect, slowing their perception of the flow of time. These were rich intervals in terms of the pleasure taken in the absence of pain. Certain authorities might count this accomplishment as a pinnacle of success for simple human beings searching for happiness in their lives. A practiced art among these folk, loafing thus could be counted as a pastime of champions. The fact remains, however, that Roy and Titus never expressed an interest in being happy, or living longer, healthier lives.

As regular shipmates, Roy and Titus were totally at ease with each other. Yarning together at home or with fellow loafers at The Shop, or making their way to and from AB's, their relationship was amicable and occasionally quite animated. Such was the mesh of their common feelings and experiences.

In the 1940s and '50s both men sailed on various vessels of Willoughby Ritcey's fleet out of Riverport under the aegis of the Riverport Shipping Company. Although Titus and Roy sailed on many different ships, Roy's favourite was the *Sally Irene*. Titus's was perhaps the *Clyde Valley*.

According to common practice among Grand Banks fishermen, Roy owned a modest financial stake in the *Sally Irene*, to get a little extra for his efforts as a doryman. The established co-operative system divided a schooner into sixty-four shares, which could be owned by fishermen, builders, or anyone else who cared to invest. Profits realized from a trip would be divided proportionately among the shareholders. Roy was happy enough with the returns on his investment, because while WR was in charge, business thrived. Titus missed out on such perks, for he had no head whatsoever for business.

As a boy, I always thought of Roy as Popeye, a favourite cartoon character at the time, but my respect for the man was totally genuine. His constant roll-your-own cigarette or pipe clenched between his teeth contributed to this impression, likewise his rolled-up sleeves and sturdy build. His wife, Letoile, hardly fit the picture of Popeye's wife (girlfriend?), Olive Oyl, though like her husband, Letoile never failed to welcome visitors, especially children. The fact is, all members of our respective families saw a good deal of each other.

* * * * *

"So how are you and Helen settlin' in to your new home?" Roy asks, as he and Titus meet roadside beside the house. Together they set out to walk the short distance up to The Shop.

"Oh, pretty good. After we heard Himmelman had it up for sale, I contacted him and we managed to strike a deal. Helen seems happy enough, but she's still not a hundred percent after our accident. Neither am I, for that matter."

"You mean the accident you two had in that fancy new Pontiac that Helen won a while back? Didn't realize you were so banged up. That was just after you got married, wasn't it?"

"Yeah, we had to stay with her parents for a couple of weeks 'til we got over the worst of it. But I tell you, it's been one thing after another since she won that car."

"I heard she got it through a contest run by *The Halifax Herald*."

"Yeah, a two-door sedan. She sold more subscriptions to the newspaper than anybody else in the province. But after she won the thing, we didn't know how to drive it. Spinny, her brother, did his best to teach her and me, but neither one of us was all that comfortable at the wheel. Half the time you got to crank it to get it goin', and they're big machines to handle."

"It's dangerous too, on the road these days," Roy says. "I read a week or so ago that since May of this year the number of accidents in the province is up over thirty percent over last year. Almost five hundred in the last six months it said, thirty-two deaths, and I don't know how many injured. Don't know but they might ha' counted you and you wife among the injured."

"If they didn't, they should have," Titus growls.

"I'm not surprised at the numbers, you. The way those young fools drive around in their big cars after a rum-runnin' trip is enough to keep a sane person off the road altogether."

"Spinny's a good example. He's smashed up a couple of cars already. Doesn't worry about that … just goes out and buys a new one after pretty well every trip."

"Is that so?"

"Well, we won't be drivin' for a while. No way can we afford to run a motor car, let alone buy one. Like I said, it's been one thing after another. I couldn't make a go of it as a farm worker out west due to drought conditions. The fella I worked for up and quit the whole operation. After that, I went down to the States for a while lookin' around. Helen had a good teaching job down there at the time. If I'd ha' got a job, we might ha' ended up stayin' down there."

"Nothing doing for you, eh?"

"Not for me there isn't. Looks like I'll go back to fishin'. Not a whole lot of choice, really. Guess I'll stay on the water. I should be ready to go on the spring trip. I can handle cookin' on the vessels."

"Yes, that's true. We've been shipmates on a couple of trips already. The men speak well of you."

"Well, that's somethin'."

"I've seen some dirty weather, but them storms were far and away the worst of all. They took a terrible toll. Four ships lost and eighty men gone last year, most of 'em with young families. An' we know most of 'em. Sad. Worse than the gales of '26. There's no escapin' the weather. You never can tell for sure. We lost a lot of good men," Roy was saying as they entered The Shop.

"What good men are you talkin' about now?" asks Austin Wamboldt, ever alert for issue and argument.

"Oh, we was talkin' about the August gales. And the luck of the draw, dependin' on the vessel you happen to ship on."

"Yes, that too," says Titus, hoping to avoid any confrontation with Austin, who he considers overly religious and bound to invoke a role for the Almighty in any and all disasters. The Great War had taught Titus otherwise, though he was not given to lecturing about it.

Around the pot-bellied stove a quorum of loafers had already gathered. For a time, the conversation rambled along about the local economy. Prompted by the remarks of Roy and Titus about the August gales, Austin meets with no opposition as he raises the topic again. Storms were an integral part of life in this community. Frank says the ship he was on returned from the Banks a week before the 1927 disaster. Amos admits he was at sea at the time but was not right in the storm.

"No," Amos Crouse says, "we knew there was a storm somewhere, but we weren't even near the Banks. I was just startin' out then. We was fishin' with Captain Harold Corkum out of Labrador that summer to see if there was any fish in that area. But we felt the swell of that August gale. It was only when we came back that we found out what was goin' on, what vessels and what crews. I was on, I think it was the *Alsatian*, with Captain Harold Corkum."

"Well, I didn't miss it, that much I know," says Roy, feeling a sudden urge to relate his experience, more as a cathartic exercise than to entertain his fellows.

"What ship were you on?" Willy Kaizer asks.

"*Andrava*, with Rollie Knickle."

"You went with him a lot, didn't you?"

"Yes, I did. Best kind of captain. He started out at age ten as catchie with his father, Captain C. John Knickle. As captain, Rollie always tries to do right by the men. Stands up for 'em and the like a' that. It was no fault of his we got caught up in that mess off a' Sable. No one saw it comin' 'til the last minute."

"Tell us about it, Roy," several of the loafers urge.

"Rollie, he gave a good account of it in the *Progress-Enterprise* just after we made it ashore. Didn't you see that?"

"Yes, but we'd like to hear it from you."

"I can give it a try," says Roy, pausing to gather himself together. "It all started after we left Canso, like the captain said. We'd taken on a load of bait and were off to fish Banquereau, southeast of Sable Island. It was a Thursday, the twenty-third of August. I'll never forget it. The weather was fine as could be when we set out.

"So there we were, the next day, late afternoon, passin' by Sable when the sky turned black as pitch. And the wind, it started gettin' up. Lemmy Eisnor, the mate from over in Mahone Bay, he told the captain we were likely in for a bit of a breeze. And sure enough, we were for it. The captain, he straightaway changed our course for the westward, hoping to avoid being blown ashore. An' we managed to make it a few miles to the southwest of Sable before the storm had its way with us. We shortened sail and hove to under double-reefed foresail. We gave up tryin' to go anywhere, 'cept the drift was carrying us slowly leeward."

"Whereabouts was the ship by this time?"

"Near as could tell by dead reckoning, we was a few miles – maybe ten or so – southwest of the main light. 'Course you couldn't see it under those conditions. We couldn't see much of anything by that time. That was as far as we made it. An' the noise, dear God, it was like all hell breakin' loose. The wind continued to build up, screechin' an' howlin' through the rigging. The ship was crackin' and creakin' like as if she'd break in half. She was like a wild animal, gone right crazy. Mountainous seas, you, mountainous, an' all in the black o' night!

"An hour or so later the foresail blew out and away. We tried to set the storm sail and jumbo, but no luck. Then a huge wave crashed down on deck. A miracle it was, no one was washed overboard. One man was knocked down, Austin Knickle, the captain's cousin, I think, he got his leg broken. But he managed to catch himself in the chains and held on.

"Then, they say, the whole chain locker upset, coverin' him with all that heavy chain. I didn't see that, but they say it was that anchored him to the ship. Otherwise he'd ha' been a goner for sure. He took an awful beatin' before he could be rescued hours later. We did our best to care for him in the fo'c'sle but there wasn't much anybody could do down there but try and hang on.

"By midnight, all the dories were carried away. There was no sign of the mainsail. And the main gaff was broke in two. All this while, we're drifting north towards the island at two to three miles an hour. That's with the rope hawser anchor out an' all. Could ha' tried both anchors, I suppose, but it wouldn't ha' made much difference. No hold on the sandy bottom, you.

"The captain had sent most of the men below by this time so's we wouldn't be washed overboard. There was nothin' to do but hold on, best we could, in the fo'c'sle, wonderin' how it's all goin' to end. But we had trouble gettin' the hatch closed, so a lot of water got into her. We couldn't do much good on deck. The mate, he volunteered to stay on as helmsman, so he was up there pretty much by hisself, lashed to the wheel."

"Brave man," someone says in an undertone.

"Well, yes, but there's many a man prefers to die above deck if they got a choice. It don't matter none to me. Anyways, we was no sooner below deck when she heeled over on her beam ends. And there she stayed, believe it or not, it must have been five minutes or more – crosstrees touchin' the water. All the time, us hanging on for dear life to anything we could get hold of, sloshin' around like rags in the fo'c'sle, waist deep in water."

"What was you all thinkin' as this was goin' on?"

"We figured the end was near. All the work in the world won't help you if your time has come. What's it like at the end? Men drown … it's the same for every man jack. We did more prayin' than thinkin' that night. It's not something I'll ever forget."

"Five minutes on her beam ends!"

"Seemed more like a lifetime. A lot of prayin' goin' on down there, I can tell you. Old Elias Walters said you'd find very few atheists in the fo'c'sle during a hurricane at sea, an' he was right. It was one big prayer meetin' down there.

"Back in the wheelhouse, the captain, he didn't have it much better, but he might have know'd a bit more 'bout what was goin' on. Can't say as whether or not he prayed, but at least he had a light. According to the paper, he said he used that to estimate the ship's position."

"How'd he do that?"

"Well, as the lamp kept burning, he kept his eye on it and saw it burn perpendicular to its normal upright position. Except for that light he had it no better than us. See, the wheel-house was also half-filled with water.

'All this while, Lemmy Eisnor was hangin' onto the helm on the open deck, pounded by one sea after another. Don't know how he managed, with all that and the ship jerkin' around like a wild bull."

"Some kind of miracle." AB speaks for all listeners.

"You're right," says Roy, "but the real miracle was when *Andrava* slowly set about rightin' herself. It took us a while to realize what was happenin'. But we was still in the thick of things, driftin' closer and closer to the west bar. So the captain, he took the fire axe and cut the anchor rope. At that, she swung free like a horse, and away we went downwind. He saw we'd have to make a run for it, and pray to God she'd make it over the bar. It was all or nothin'.

"Well, sir, I'm tellin' you, we struck bottom at least five or six times on the way over. There was no more 'n ten fathom under her keel at the best of times, but somehow she rutsched her way acrost. Once on the other side the wind eased off a little and we was able to man the pumps. She was listin' badly."

"About what time o' day was this?"

"Oh, I'd guess it was around two or three in the morning before we was able to breathe a bit easier and look to helpin' them what was injured. Soon as we began to see the light a' day the captain, he called upon all hands to clear away the wreckage. To help lighten her we threw all our bait over the side. And sand! There was sand everywhere and in everything. We used shovels to clear it from the deck. By this time, it was all we could do to haul ourselves around. Cookie, he managed – I don't know to this day how he did it – to get a pot of coffee goin' so's we could all have a mug-up."

'That was a welcome break, I'll bet," says Frank, to which comment Roy simply nods. Despite the tale he tells, he's not someone readily given to hyperbole, or, for that matter, to swearing.

"Last thing we did was we turned to and manhandled the cable back on board. See, most of the cable left on board washed over the side and was trailin' after like a sea anchor. That helped save us. It took us a while to haul that cable back on board. We was pretty well used up. We thought we'd die if we didn't get a real mug-up. Most of the riggin' was still in place, so we dug out a spare main topsail and bent it on as a storm sail. With that, and a jib and a staysail, we headed for home. It was gettin' on towards midnight four days later, on the Saturday, we made it into Lunenburg."

Logging Legends (October 1929)

"Looks like we'll get an early start on our wood this year," says Roy as they relax in AB's on a cool fall evening in early October 1929.

Titus replies, "Yes, it's been a fairly good season. I heard the highliner landed over five thousand quintal. That was Joey Wentzell, out of Riverport. The Lunenburg crowd did pretty well too."

"Some ships are already ashore being overhauled, and they're gearing up for next year. Why don't we team up again like last fall and cut ourselves five or six cord apiece? I've got a good stand up behind Perry's Hill, and there's your piece up behind Danny's. You and me could also cut a load apiece on the Commons. We're allowed that. An' we'll use my ox team."

"Good enough, let's do it. Someone else, maybe Frank here, might want to join in."

"Yeah, that'll work for me," says Frank Zinck, adding, "Roy's team will be handy, then later on, what's his name ... Mosher, out there in Kingsburg, has a gas-powered portable saw he loans out. That will make the job a whole lot easier. Depends of course on the price he wants, but I can ask him on Sunday."

"Either that or go cold," AB puts in from his seat by the counter. "I used to work winters for Davison Lumber, up in the country. A lot of us did that in the fall of the year."

"That way at least a man could be more or less guaranteed of makin' a wage in the off season," says Frank.

"As good or better than fishin'," says AB.

"Next thing you'll be tellin' us all about logging."

"Well, I reckon I could," AB replies.

"Go 'way, Arthur, you mean to say you used to be in the loggin' business?" says Willy.

"Well, I was, in a way. I worked in logging camps for about five winters after I got married."

"Five winters!" exclaims Roy. "Tell us about it. This I gotta hear."

"Davison had a lot of camps and mills up in Annapolis County. I worked mostly as cook at a place called Crossburn, up beyond New Germany, near the headwaters of the LaHave River. Davison went out of business just after the war. Head Office was in New York, but the district office was in Bridgewater. All the work of course was done out in the woods."

"Don't hear much 'bout Davison these days," says Roy.

"No, everything was sold off nearly ten years ago, back in about '21. I don't imagine there's much left of Crossburn now, but when I left in 1916, it was a going concern. It was Davison's Camp #1 – a small town really, bigger than Rose Bay. It was the company's HQ for the logging and the railway business. It had everything: a couple of dozen houses, post office, school, doctor, a roundhouse for company trains, stables, cookhouse, and even a general store."

"A wee bit bigger than Rose Bay," says Frank.

"Everything but a church," says AB, nodding his assent. "But I remember a young Baptist minister, Allen White, used to visit the camps on Sundays, by train if you please, along with a ladies choir."

"A ladies choir!" exclaim all of the loafers, shaken wider awake than usual by this revelation.

"Why, yes," says AB. "I daresay those loggers were better behaved in the woods than you lot are when you're left out there on your own. The company had pretty strict rules. For one thing, no liquor was allowed."

"No liquor!" Again, the chorus of astonishment.

"I even had Carrie up with me at first for a little while at some camps near Gold River. Later on the company moved me up to Annapolis and Kings counties. Here, hang on a moment, and I'll fetch a couple of photos I brought along to show you. I've got them right here behind the counter. This one was taken of the sawmill in Crossburn. Here was where all the lumber was produced for constructing the town and for supplying the outlying lumber camps."

"Looks like you'd have your hands full feeding all those men – not a soft job like on a schooner, eh, Titus," says Roy, giving his neighbour a friendly jab in the side.

"And I can tell you, very little food got wasted," AB adds proudly. "Camp superintendent was a fellow by the name of Cross. He was the camp boss – a real nice fellow – but he wasn't happy unless I could keep the cost under fifty cents a man per day. I think the horses got more."

"'Course, that was wartime," says Titus, lighting up a tailor-made Players.

"An' here's another photo. I only have two. This one is from Moose Lake Junction, another of the logging camps I worked at up in Kings County. The train was part of the Springfield Railway, owned by Davison. It's just one of half a dozen trains they had – miles and miles of rail. Davison Lumber was a huge operation, they employed hundreds of men. But the biggest place was Hastings. It's a long story, but I believe it's been bought out completely by another American outfit. The heyday of logging lasted until July 1921, when Davison's whistle blew for the last time."

"You mean to say you cooked for all those men?" Titus asks, peering at the numbers with an unmistakable touch of fresh respect for this congenial storekeeper. He cannot help

Mill workers and their cook AB (in a white shirt and apron) at a mill near Cross-burn. Collars and ties are suggestive of a visitor's day.

This photograph shows a typical portable Davison Lumber Camp (#22) at Moose Lake (now known as Palmer Lake), Kings County. The train is a Pittsburg Locomotive #2 of the Springfield Railway.

comparing what he sees in the photo with his job as a sea cook. AB nods in the affirmative. No further proof of past performance is called for in this challenging field.

"Mind you, at Moose Lake Junction I had a young flunky to help out peeling spuds and the like, and Carrie was with me once in a while towards the end. See, the company had accommodation for married couples in most of the camps. They weren't all that primitive, you know, the camps, I mean. One of my biggest jobs was preparing lunches for the men to take out in the woods. We had a couple of young fellows whose job it was to carry the lunches out to work sites every day – all except on Sundays of course. I used to pack the lunches in ash-splint baskets made by the Indians."

"I expect Davison thinned out the trees a fair bit too. Not much left, all clear-cut, I suppose," Willy offers, expecting no argument.

"It pretty much was, I'm afraid to say. Might grow back in a hundred years or so, but there wasn't a whole lot of trees left standing at the end of it. An article I saw in the *Bulletin* said theirs was the biggest operation in North America back at the turn of the century."

"Well, good for them," says Frank. "Guess we should be thankful there's more than enough left around here for us."

"What did you do after loggin'?" Austin asks.

"I worked as cook for Imperial Oil over in Woodside, in Dartmouth. They were constructing the oil refinery at the time … completed in early '18. I retired from there about that time and came home here."

"You must have been on that job at the time of the explosion."

"Yes, I was. The company did what it could to help in the rescue efforts. But we didn't have much damage to deal with on site."

"Nobody killed?"

"No."

"Lucky," says Frank. "Lehman Wentzell told me an interesting story about when he was on the *Niobe*. She was in Halifax at the time of the explosion, see, and I think he must ha' been an officer on board of her. She'd been taken out of service other than serving as a Maritime HQ for administration. Apparently she wasn't much good for anything else … an old ship, outdated."

"*Niobe*, wasn't she one of our ships served to blockade German ships from American ports during the war?" asks Titus.

"Yes," says AB, "but *Niobe* was considered obsolete, a leftover if you can believe it, from the Boer War. She was an old Royal Navy four-stacker, taken out of service early in the war to become the depot ship. Moored at Pier 4 as naval HQ in Halifax, she was a base of administration for our coastal patrols and training centre. But really, those people had no control over what went on in terms of traffic in and out of the harbour, even though Canadian 'authorities' were supposed to be in charge. Halifax pilots, working independently, were really the ones doing the day-to-day work."

"So what's Lehman's story? He's postmaster in Riverport now. But he was in the navy during the war, wasn't he?" says Austin.

"Yeah, Lehman lost his arm in action at sea early in the war. They must have given him an easier job after that on the *Niobe*. He married Annie Moore. She's a war bride from Wales. They got two boys, Ronald and Allan."

"Just like in the army, patch 'em up and send 'em back out again," says Titus.

"So, what about the *Niobe*?" Austin demands impatiently.

"Hang on, for goodness sake, I'm comin' to that," says Frank. "He says he was on her on the morning of the explosion, in the mess room with a couple of shipmates. And one of his buddies, who arrived a bit later than the others, when he learned there was a ship on fire in the harbor, couldn't wait to see what was going on. So he ran to the nearest porthole, opened it, and stuck his head out. Trouble was, at that very moment the *Mont-Blanc* blew up. Lehman said the man's head was blown clean off, the rest of his body fell back on the mess room floor."

"You're makin' this up," says Willy.

"You can't make up this kind of stuff," Frank retorts. "Ask Lehman if you don't believe me! It probably wasn't the first time he saw a man's head blown off anyway. Where have you been all your life?"

"Still for all, it's better than survivin' with half your head blown off," says Austin.

"Whooo, what a way to go ...," someone mutters.

"Bad luck ... painless, though," adds another.

"Lehman said the *Niobe* suffered some damage in the blast. And seven of her crew took a pinnace to the ship loaded with munitions. They were goin' to put a tow line on her, but it blew up as they boarded and killed 'em. *Niobe* took a lot of damage, and some on board her died."

"You never know when your time is up. All things considered ...," says Austin, about to assume preaching mode.

"That reminds me, gentlemen, time's up, I'm closing shop," says AB.

Rush to Marriage (ca. 1934)

Through work at The Shop, AB pretty much was able to keep tabs on goings-on in the community at large. So he wasn't surprised to see young Amos Crouse show up from time to time. Amos hailed from nearby Crouse's Settlement. But he seemed to be spending much of his spare time in Riverport and District, more specifically the seaport town of Riverport. The prime attraction was Marion Lohnes, a young lady adopted as a foster child by a childless couple, Gabriel Zinck and his wife Jenny. Gabby was the locally famous proprietor of a combined barber shop and ice cream parlour precariously perched on the waterfront.

"Evening, Amos," says AB, welcoming the young man to join the several loafers already convened. Amos's courteous response was duly returned to one and all before he made a few small purchases, some cigarettes and pop, which, in effect, constituted his admission to the club. He did not intend to remain long, as the topic under discussion apparently concerned harvesting, a theme in which Amos had little interest. But sure enough, before he made it to the door, the topic of fishing came up again.

"I guess you'd be thinking that fishing is a more dangerous business than rum-runnin' after what you've been just through," says Frank, who spoke up before Amos could escape relating his recent adventure. Like many young men, Amos had spent time on various rum-runners during Prohibition days, although according to the little he ever revealed about that particular pursuit, it was pretty tame stuff.

"There isn't much to rum-runnin', though it pays better than fishin'," says Amos. "I expect you all know that. You had a contact on shore, and a wireless on board. The speedboats came out to where you was to load up. Nothing to do but sitting around, eating, sleeping, playing cards – never had any run-ins with the law at all. Saw a few Coast Guard vessels, but we never got too close. Steam away, keep clear of 'em, long as we was way out beyond the twelve-mile limit – that's international waters – they didn't bother you."

"No excitement at all?" asks Frank.

"One time we left Bermuda to go around to the American coast. We broke down and drifted around in the Gulf Stream for three or four weeks. I wouldn't call that very exciting. Another rum-runner eventually found us and towed us back to Bermuda. So we had two or three weeks there while we had a new shaft put in. No, not a whole lot of excitement."

"Dory fishin' provides more than enough excitement for me," says William. "The only problem is there's a lot more hard work involved than in rum-running. Me and my dory-mate were lucky to make it back alive one trip last spring."

"What happened?" asks Roy, who had spent the better part of his working life as a doryman.

"Well, I'm sure that you, of all people, know what that braided rope is for that hangs from the plug on the bottom of a dory. Well, for those of you who don't, it's a life-saving device. And now I'll tell you how it works. We completed our run, see, and had just started to make our way back to the vessel. We had good load of cod on board. The only trouble was there was a cross sea running. A sea hit us and bingo! The dory went bottom up, dumpin' everything out of her, us included."

"You must ha' been able to swim, otherwise you wouldn't be here," says Austin.

"No, I can't swim, but see, there was so much air trapped in my oilskins that I didn't sink. So I dog-paddled my way back to the dory. I looked all around but couldn't see my dorymate anywhere. What I did see was that length of braided rope attached to the bottom of the dory. I grabbed on to that, and managed to pull myself up on top. Next thing I heard this voice comin' from underneath the dory sayin', 'Jasus, Billy, don't crawl up on top of 'er. I'm under here.' So I hung on to the rope, and I guess he was holdin' on to the sides of the dory afeard to let go lest he'd sink. It took me all of fifteen or twenty minutes before I could convince him to put his face in the water and come out from under the dory. I might have mentioned seeing a shark nearby. That did the job."

"What did you do then?"

"We hung on for our lives all night long on the bottom of that overturned dory. The vessel found us early next morning."

* * * * *

"So, Amos, what about your latest adventure?" asks Frank, getting straight to the question he'd been waiting to bring up. "Sounds like from what little the papers report, you fellows had a pretty exciting time of it on the *Astrid W*. That was around about mid-summer, wasn't it?"

"Yes," says Amos, "we was lucky to make it ashore. We only had about twenty minutes before she went down."

"Whereabouts was that?"

"Between Grand Banks and Baccaro Bank, in what they call the Gully, deep water about 1,700 fathoms down. We had about 13,000 pounds of halibut on board."

"How many men was aboard?" asks Frank.

"There was fourteen of us. But like I said, no one was lost."

"We heard the trouble began with an explosion. What exactly was it that happened anyway?"

"Most of us were below deck, either in our bunks or having breakfast at the time. This was very early in the morning. Brad Whynacht of Lunenburg was on watch, and the explosion blew a hole in the side of the schooner where he was standing – the deck was all torn up. Blew his oilskins right off him and cut him up pretty bad on his hands and face. It was the air tank that blew. Don't know why, but there's no relief valve on them, you know. We woke up fast enough and found ourselves looking out on the water. A couple of us got banged up pretty good."

"How about the captain?" someone asks.

"No, the captain, Walter Crouse, he wasn't hurt much, and he got us off the ship pretty quick. But Whynacht was in bad shape."

"Is the captain your father?"

"No, he's no direct relation. My father is John Crouse – never been to sea in his life."

"A wise man, your father," says Frank, a point no one was about to dispute.

"It was all we could do to get three dories over the side before she went down. But at times like that you just do what comes natural. You get off soon as you can when the boat's goin' down. We had no time at all to get food and water; fourteen of us in all. So for the next five days we rowed and sailed best we could. We was about 125 miles southeast of Sable Island."

"What kind of weather did you have?"

"Not too bad, fairly rough seas, but fog and rain set in, and after two days one of the dories separated. In two dories then, we tried to make Sable Island. Unfortunately, that didn't work out so we kept on for the mainland.

"Fog and rain! Fog and rain! Thick o' fog the whole five days. That was the worst of it. Would ha' been clear weather, wouldn't ha' been so bad. Not a good feeling. Pretty hard to set down here and describe it – what you feel, wonderin' whether somebody'll come along and pick you up. But I guess some of you know what I mean. A couple of times we heard the sound of engines in the distance, but they went by without seein' us. The closest land was Cape Breton, and that was close on 150 miles away."

"Whereabouts did you make landfall?" asks Roy.

"On Sunday, we sailed into Little Anse on Cape Breton. The men come out and towed us in. We were in pretty bad shape and found it hard to walk. The people there were very good to us. After good food and rest, we made it home by train."

"You was lucky no one was badly hurt," says Frank.

"Well, Norman Conrad was in hospital for quite a while, and the captain's knee was damaged, and Brad lost an eye."

"There'd be some compensation for that, I'd imagine," offers AB.

"Brad was offered the choice of two dollars a month for life or a straight out two hundred dollars cash for his loss."

"What did he take?"

"The two hundred."

"Not much for an eye."

"Better than nothin', I'd say." This from Roy, who had been a seasoned doryman when Amos was in diapers.

"You might want to go back to bottle fishing for a while after that halibutin' trip," Carmen Creaser puts in quickly. "I might be able to get you a place if you're interested."

"I don't think so. But thanks anyway. I tried it for a while back in the late '20s. First trip I made was with Moyle Crouse on the *Selma K*. We sailed to St. Pierre and loaded 3,800 cases of whisky and headed straight to Nantucket. There wasn't much to it. We just made sure we was always just beyond the twelve-mile limit or a little further than that. Speedboats used to come out and take it off of us, a couple of hundred cases at a time. And they'd run it in. That would be the last you'd see of them 'til maybe the next time. Not a whole lot of excitement there. Anyways, we were young and foolish, and when you're eighteen, you don't worry about danger. We were makin' good money."

"There's still money to be made up here in the Maritimes," says Carmen.

"I'm sure you two young fellas can work somethin' out," says Frank. "Just don't let Machine Gun Kelly catch up with you."

"So when are you getting married, Amos?" asks AB, sensing that the time had come for a change of topic.

"Oh, who have you got your eye on, Amos?" asks Carmen, pretending a sudden interest in Amos's love life, whereas in fact Amos's courting activity was common knowledge in the community.

"Oh, didn't you know? Lately he's been hanging around Gabriel's Ice Cream Parlour and Barber Shop," says Willy Kaizer, who had seen Amos in company there with Miss Marion, the pretty adopted daughter of Gabby and Jenny Zinck.

"Is that so now?" Carmen says to Amos, who by this time appears thoroughly embarrassed. "You better act fast if you want results."

"What do you mean?" asks Amos, shaken out of his trance by this fresh challenge to his wits.

"I didn't see you at the dance last Saturday at the IOOF hall."

"What's that got to do with anything? I was at sea. After the *Astrid W.* went down, we came home and I signed onto another boat to finish my summer fishing."

"Foolish man. Well, too bad, but you should know by now you got some competition for Marion's hand."

"Go 'way, now, who might that be?" says Roy, curiosity piqued by this soap opera intrigue.

"Why, none other than The Yodelling Ranger," Carmen replies. "Least that's what Hank Snow calls himself these days. I saw him dancing with Marion that evening, and," Carmen adds after a significant pause, "he even walked her home."

"They say Hank's a lady's man," said Willy, "but I like Wilf Carter better."

"You maybe ought to take some time off fishing, Amos. Stick around home for a while," says Carmen, rubbing the sore spot. "Come on rum-runnin' with me an' you won't have to spend so much time at sea ... and you'll make more money."

"I suppose it might help if I learned to yodel as well," Amos says, realizing there was no easy way out of the situation other than to join in on the joke. But he didn't plan to waste any time making his way to Gabby's Ice Cream Parlour.

Running the Rum (1935)

Despite the fact Captain Timothy Haliburton Himmelman lived next door, and could tell a yarn as well or better than any old sea dog, he seldom showed up on an evening when loafers held shop. However, Bertie patronized The Shop for many of his regular groceries, exercising undue parsimony in the process, as AB couldn't help but observe. All too often the old captain needed reminding of credit overdue.

Himmelman families almost invariably "belonged" to the Lutheran Church. This evening Bertie and AB were in the midst of a light discussion about the new minister of the Rose Bay Evangelical Lutheran Church as Willy Kaizer and Frank Zinck make their way into The Shop.

Bertie's cousin, Reverend George Lawrence Himmelman, substituted for Reverend Harry N. Lossing, the regular minister, when home one summer in the early '30s on a visit. "Yes," Bertie was saying, "Lawrence started off young, practisin' his preachin' and the like all the time, even in the Crossroads Store – well before you started up here, Arthur. Couldn't ha' been over twelve years old at the time. I remember he used to rig up in a black cloak and practise right in his mother's store. Jediah was very religious, so she didn't mind at all. And Lawrence, he used to perform a burial service for any dead animals he found. When Mr. Slaunwhite's dog Bob died of old age, Lawrence could see the old fellow was all cut up about it. So what does he do? He goes ahead and preaches a memorial sermon right there beside the dog."

"That would have been a eulogy. I guess young Lawrence was trying to make sense of the world and express his love of life – interesting. Do you think Slaunwhite appreciated the gesture?" AB asks Bertie. But Bertie is interrupted before he can summon a reply.

"Let me guess," says Willy, with a laugh. "The sermon might have gone something like this:

> Here lies old Bob,
> Grant him peace, dear Lord,
> For he was a good dog
> And he always ate his dinner.
> Please forgive his errant ways …
> Umm … because …"

As Willy pauses to think, Frank supplies the next line:

> "For he's not a reg'lar sinner."

This piece of ad hoc poetry is rewarded with chuckles from all, except an old sea captain and a middle-aged grocer. AB says nothing but looks on the proceedings with growing disapproval. Fortunately for discipline in the room, the subject changes abruptly as Carmen Creaser bursts in with startling local news.

"'Sergeant Rennie does it again!' That's what it says right here in the *Progress*," shouts Carmen, waving the paper around. "Well, good for him!" This last bit with more than a touch of sarcasm as he holds up the page of printed proof. The talk this winter evening in The Shop continues with news of a recent RCMP seizure of a cache of booze uncovered in Riverport.

"It wasn't your cache, Carmen, so why worry?" says Frank. "They're bound to come up with the odd find every now and again. There's hides all over the place – in barns, outhouses, sheds, along the shore, out in the woods. The cops can't be everywhere."

"How much did they find this time?" asks Willy.

"Sixty-three kegs, valued at four thousand five hundred dollars, they say. Found in the woods in Riverport. Here, I'll read it to you. 'It was a large place tunneled in the ground and the roof was kept up and had a trap door in it. The hideout resembled a mine. The RCMP arrived at 9 o'clock Wednesday morning and they were until six removing the liquor. It had to be boated out of the woods and then placed on a truck. An arrest is expected to be made shortly.'"

"You better make a run for it, Carmen, while there's still time," says Frank.

"Oh, the cops always say that. Makes it look like they know what they're doin'."

"Sounds like the kind of hide what's his name, Shillelagh, over there on the north side, used last year over on Parks Island," says Willy.

"Could be anywheres along Oxner's Beach too, north or south from WR's cottage. Who knows … but they keep a pretty steady lookout along that stretch."

"How much is there in one keg, anyway?" Roy interrupts.

"Five gallons," says Willy, "more than enough to keep your spirits up for a month or so."

"WR's active all along the Atlantic seaboard I hear tell, including the Bay of Fundy and even the Gulf of St Lawrence," says Frank. "Carmen here, he knows how it works, don't you, Carmen?"

"Tell us how it works, Carmen." A chorus of voices assails the young man's easily weakened senses of propriety. A well-known fisherman from Riverport, turned rum-runner, Carmen is still active in the trade despite the end of Prohibition two years earlier. The drug of youth, spiked with a few drops of booze, spurs him on impulse to storytelling.

"I think you already know more than enough about how

it works around here. But I can tell you how it worked down in the States a few years ago. See, I got a late start back in '29. The American coast was a lot better than this coast. We got a lot better pay, and there was nothing to the work."

No stopping the young fool now, AB thinks, as he watches Carmen make himself comfortable. Although not averse to a ceremonial drink at Christmas when a bottle of something or other may be passed around in the grandparent Wentzell's house, AB never drank at home. Nor was he known to smoke. Unlike his friend and counterpart Charles Zellers in Feltzen South, he does not allow loafers to keep a jug of their own booze out of sight behind his store counter. Not that loafers in Zellers' store reserved their rum for themselves – quite the contrary. Every practitioner at Zellers' establishment was more than agreeable to share and share alike with his fellows. There never seemed to be a shortage of the stuff outside of home settings. But Zellers' store was not The Shop. Such hijinks were not allowed in The Shop, a location generally acknowledged as "dry." There were of course no restrictions on smoking. In consequence more than once, returning to his home smelling like an ashtray, AB might have been accused by his wife of indulging.

"How much would you get paid for a trip?" asks Roy, who had never been involved in rum-running – not a squealer certainly, for he enjoyed a drink as well as the next man among the gathering that evening, excepting of course the proprietor.

"On the American coast at that time, we got eighty dollars a month – if you got clear of the cargo. See, every three weeks – we only worked dark nights, we always worked the moon – dark nights, if we managed to offload our booze, our wages was eighty a month and a hundred and forty-five dollar bonus."

"That's more than you ever see from fishin', even now," says Roy, "and a bonus on top!"

"That's if we got clear of the load that month," Carmen repeats.

"So the bonus was more than the month's wages …," says Roy, as he ponders the scandalous wage disparity. Yet it was something he had heard about time and time again during his years at sea. It was too late for him now of course, but why had he listened to his wife?

"Oh, the bonus was always a lot more than what the wages was, but we always got clear. But here on this coast, we get nothin' here on this coast. Here, all we get is thirty-five dollars a month. A year or so ago a Mountie boat cornered us just offshore Lunenburg. He run about thirty mile an hour, an' all we could do was eight. He could steam circles around us. He wanted us to stop but we didn't stop – we didn't care. All we got was thirty-five dollars a month. We used to go and lie down on the engine-room floor, an' the old man, he was the one makin' the money, he took the wheel.

"They'd just steam up and try to get aboard us, but the wash from our boat used to keep the fella away. He couldn't get aboard, and when we got outside where the water was rough, he'd give it up for a bad job. That happened to us three or four times. You see, we had what you call a mother ship. We never went far after rum. We just went off to the mother ship anchored on LaHave Bank."

"So you were a go-between – you would pick it up off another ship?"

"We'd just pick it up off a mother ship at LaHave Bank."

"Do you recall the name of the mother ship?"

"Um … *Tessie* … *Tessie* something. Sometimes they'd hire one of the ordinary fishermen out on a charter trip. They used to anchor right on LaHave Bank."

"Oh, that would have to be the *Tessie Audrey*, wouldn't it?"

"Yeah, that's the one, *Tessie Audrey*."

"That was your ship at one time, wasn't it, Bertie?"

"He shouldn't be so damned nosy," mutters Bertie, who up to this point remained tight-lipped.

"What's there to worry about, Bertie? That's all ancient history now," says Frank.

"Tell us about it, Bertie. Who were you workin' for?" says Carmen, who likes to get people goin', get under their skin if he can manage it. But Bertie, already on his feet and headed for the door, is having none of it.

"He's been well sworn to secrecy, no doubt about it," says Frank, as Bertie slams the door on the issue and heads off up the road.

"I had no idea he was so religious," says Carmen, "but there's no harm talkin' about it now. Those days are pretty much over, though it used to be the way of things around here."

"Perhaps we can test him out another time when he's in a better mood," offers Titus. "But it's best to be careful around him. I once heard he threw a man overboard in a rage, during a fight at sea – might have been on that same ship."

"No, you got that wrong, Titus," says Roy. "He didn't throw the man overboard. The man was three-quarters drunk, and he fell overboard. And it wasn't the *Tessie Audrey*."

"How do you know that?"

"Well, I didn't sail with Captain Bertie on that trip. But I know a couple of the men who did. Bertie's nephew was one. They was on the *Giant King* that time, comin' back with a load of salt from Turks Islands," says Roy. "She was a new vessel built over there in West LaHave."

"So what happened, was there a fight between Bertie and one of the crew?"

"That's what I understand. Bertie never talks about it, and I don't think it's even worth askin' him. But according to the story I heard he deserves a lot of credit."

"And what exactly was it that he was supposed to have done?" Austin asks.

"They was only a day out from Turks, and the mate, Robert Himmelman, was nursing some sort of grudge over something that took place before they left port. I think he's Bertie's nephew ... Long Albert's son. He was nursing his grudge with booze, and had such a jag on that evening he began slashing with his sheath knife at any riggin' he was able to reach. First he cut the main boom ropes. You can imagine the result."

"He must have been right out of his mind … crazy as a coot," says Willy.

"Yes, you'd have to think so. But Bertie followed him up and knocked him into the scuppers. You don't want to tangle with Bertie. He can be a cranky old fella sometimes. You durst not cross him. He's a different cut from the rest of the Himmelman family. And he's a very big man, strong as a bull moose. Anyways, the story is that when the mate managed to stand up and lean against the rail, a sudden lurch of the ship sent him overboard. See, the ship was right out of control by this time … completely off course."

"I take it all this was goin' on down in the Caribbeans," says Austin. "So, what happened next?"

"Well, apparently a shipmate of his volunteered to go in one of the ship's boats to look for him. The captain agreed, even though it was the middle of the night, you, and away he went. The rest of the crew was busy enough trying to regain control of the ship, repairing all the riggin'."

"I'd think more 'n twice about attempting a rescue under those conditions. Wouldn't you?" says Frank.

"Good chance you'd never find either of 'em again."

"Well, that's probably what Bertie was thinkin', but the guy in the dory found the drunken fool and pulled him into the dory. He could swim, and he was lucky too. There's a lot of sharks in those waters, see. An hour or so later when Bertie was able to get the ship turned around – it had to be by pure dead reckoning – he managed to locate the two of 'em."

"So they rescued the poor bugger."

"Yes, they did," says Roy, "thanks to a smart and able captain and a brave shipmate. But it's not something you can always count on bein' rewarded for. It's just one of those things that happens at sea and no one ever hears anything more about. Bertie's probably smart to try and keep it quiet. Just don't underestimate the man. He's a veteran sea captain … he's been going to sea even longer than me. And that's sayin' somethin'. He takes after Long Albert Himmelman. They're brothers. An' besides Tommy, he had at least three other brothers – George, Allen, and Nahman – an' he had a couple of sisters as well. I forget their names.

"Titus, you must ha' been thinkin' of Long Albert. Now there's a man never shied off a fight. I heard tell of a fight once down at the old T wharf in Boston, when Long Albert threw his opponent halfways across the width of a schooner into the water. Then he turned and helped fish the fellow out. Down there they called him a 'Viking in a sou'wester.' The 'father of captains' you could say … a big man too, he was two hundred some, and over six foot in his sock feet. Why, he was master of his own ship when Angus Walters was a babe."

"Didn't he race *Independence* against the *Bluenose* in '21?'

"That he did, and after he lost to Angus he joined forces on the *Bluenose* and advised Angus where best to position ballast in the schooner. He tended the sheets with Angus in the race against *Columbia*."

"We all know how that ended."

"Yes, we do," says Willy. "*Bluenose* won the first two of the three races. The third race didn't happen."

"Only thing, the Americans on the International Racing Committee ruled *Bluenose* passed a navigation buoy on the wrong side," Frank hastens to explain.

"I heard Captain Angus didn't receive notification of the ruling before the race," says AB.

"Anyways, the trophy remained with the *Bluenose*, and the prize money was shared," says Willy. "That sort of put a drag on the whole business of racing for a few years."

"I wonder now, what Long Albert thought of the race. You know, he and all his crew was lost in a winter storm comin' back from Newfoundland in 1923 in his new schooner, *Keno*.

And she was only launched in April that same year. Can you believe it!"

"An' he wasn't even rum-runnin' at the time," says Austin.

* * * * *

"Yes, rum-runnin'," Carmen continues impatiently. "Now, where was I before old Bertie took off? Well, here on the Canadian coast it's lots more work. Oh yeah ... see, when I worked on the American coast, down in St. Pierre we'd never touch the stuff. The Frenchmen did all the work, loaded it all – whisky. This coast here, as you know, we have no whisky. Don't have no whisky at all ... all Demerera rum in five-gallon kegs ... pass me the flask."

"Rum's way better for you anyway," someone mutters, as AB focuses on wiping the counter.

"So, when you worked on the American coast, did you ever use smokescreens to try and escape from the Coast Guard?"

"Oh yeah. See, at that time you stood watch up on top of the wheelhouse with the spyglasses. You could see a cutter a long ways off. Soon as we seen anything that looked like a cutter we used to get out so they wouldn't pick us up. If they picked us up in the night, we'd use what you call a smokescreen. That worked when there was any wind, but when it's calm, she's no good. They'd put something in her, it would blow out smoke – you could almost cut it with a knife, so thick it was. See, when it was calm, it just left a bank of smoke as you steamed along. But if there was any wind, it used to blow all around, and you could get a half-hour or so to get away from them. And most rum-runners on the American coast used to steam way slower than the cutters. They had what they called four-stackers, old destroyers left over from the war, and they could steam forty or fifty knots. If they'd have picked us up, they would have had us."

"But you say you never got caught."

"No, but some of those fellas were good. I remember one trip we broke down, and it was for two weeks we had a cutter laying there alongside of us. And sometimes in the night they would just drift up, right up, I'd say about twenty feet from us, so close they was, when it was calm. One night he drifted up real close, could ha' been only ten or fifteen feet. And we took a case of whisky and slung it over his stern, and that's the last we saw of the cutter. That's all they wanted. They was mostly good fellas. If you left them alone they left you alone. That's what we found out anyway."

"I heard there was some rough stuff goin' on down there too," says Roy.

"Yeah, sometimes they would fire at us. Some of the Coast Guard fellas were pretty trigger-happy. Other times maybe just stop and yarn with us. Fire stuff at 'em – rocks and things – an' you were askin' for trouble. But it was done, I know. We heard of different boats doin' it."

"Did you ever run into Machine Gun Kelly here off our coast? He was a trigger-happy captain with the RCMP's Customs and Excise Branch."

"Oh, yeah! We had a bag of cabbages up under the whaleback, and one night this fella, Kelly, came after us. He opened up onto us with his machine gun, and if he would have fired into the wheelhouse, he would have had us. He fired his machine gun for the whaleback, and that bag of cabbages got cut up right into sauerkraut. And the best of it was we all forgot about the cook. He was in his bunk and slept right through it. He was sleeping below it, right below the whaleback, in his bunk. He didn't know anything about it. We forgot to call him. But that happened about a year before Tanner's murder last May. We've all heard about that."

"May second, that was. But your cook was lucky compared to William Tanner. Tanner was a family man from Stonehurst, near Lunenburg. Leaves a wife and four or five kids," says Willy.

"They say Tanner took his own motor boat that night to a rendezvous off Cross Island with *Muir*, WR's mother ship. The business had just been completed when Kelly turned up and took after him. Guess after his machine gun jammed, or so he said, he used a high-powered rifle to try and ignite a keg of rum on Tanner's motorboat. At least that's what the asshole told the court."

"And didn't he go and apologize for blowing the poor man's head off!" says Frank.

"The bugger was never even charged for straight-out murder," says Carmen. "Got off scot free, though he was later run out of town. With any luck, we'll never see him again."

"In the old days of Prohibition, did you go ashore in St. Pierre?" asks Roy.

"Oh yes, we knew all the cafés. We spent a lot of time at Madame Boutons. But in St. Pierre we were actually only there about two nights at the very most, while they loaded the liquor on the boats – unless bad weather, we'd stay another day. My first trip there was, oh, I'd guess, in 1929.

"I bought a car in 1931, up in Liverpool. We used to get our pay every time we'd come back into Liverpool. On the American coast, that was our base. Bought a new Chev for nine hundred dollars in Liverpool. Nine hundred! That's a sports Chev, two wheels on each side – she carried the spare wheels on each side. That was 1931. I had just turned twenty-one," says Carmen, as AB looks on in concern. By this time, there was no easy way he could decently call an end to proceedings.

As secretary of the Lutheran Church Council, Arthur Benjamin Lohnes had a certain reputation to maintain. And that wouldn't last very long should his wife Carrie or the Lutheran Church unearth evidence of "untoward" late evening activities at The Shop – and she, being Superintendent of the Junior Lutheran League … "Oh my!" he wonders, as he draws a deep breath. "Well, at least there's no swearing going on."

"We was just young fellas," Carmen continues, "and we liked the excitement and the money. The money was especially good on the American coast. We figured we was millionaires. From St. Pierre, we'd always bring back cigarettes and perfume, and chocolates with liquor inside, like rum chocolates or something. We used to know lots of girls around Liverpool – bring 'em maybe a couple of boxes of chocolates … no large amounts. It was all American cigarettes – Camels, and Luckies, and Chesterfields and all that stuff. We never brought any up to sell that I know of, except to give to our friends. The only thing we did bring large amounts of was sugar. We used to bring sugar from St. Pierre … crazy, you. We used to buy it in big twenty-five-pound bags. We'd curse it up and down. It was hard stuff to handle at night. We'd have all these bags of sugar, bring it over, you know, just for use in our own families."

"When you sat off the American coast, how did you know when a boat was comin' off to meet up?" asks Frank, who, like Roy, was another local fisherman who had no first-hand experience in rum-running.

"Wireless," answers Carmen. "Over the wireless, every day."

"You usen't be able to do that," says Roy, who recalls rather rougher days at sea when fishermen never knew what the next six hours might bring, weather-wise.

"Do what?

"Communicate by ship-to-shore radio."

"Yeah, all our boats had a wireless operator on board, and every couple of hours he was talking to shore, to agents on the shore. It was all arranged with the wireless before. The last year or two, it was handled in big shots. Then they would send out twenty or thirty men from New York. We called 'em Dukhobors. I think they were Polish. They helped handle the cargo, see. We'd have up to seven thousand cases. In summertime, we sometimes took the deck out of her so she'd hold eight thousand cases. The Americans – you could make a lot in the summertime. I know one summer we had a deck load of champagne, and in the hot sun, all you could hear was *pop! pop! pop!*"

"Were codes or something used for the messages?" is the next question from Roy, readily answered by Carmen.

"Oh yes, but it was all in code. Oh God, yes. Or the Americans would know exactly what we were doing. See, in the daytime, we lay over a hundred miles offshore. Soon as it got dark, we started steaming in. The very first trip I made was on the *Frederick H.* out of Dartmouth.

"Anyways, we had to unload all those cases one night. The Dokhobors put all that aboard one of those coal barges goin' up the harbour. Tow boats used to be towing these coal barges up and down the coast. We'd throw the booze on the coal barge. The tow boat up ahead wasn't supposed to know we were there at all. They just thought they were towing a coal barge. See, it was in the dark and you got two miles apart. Out to sea, you need a long tow line."

"So they didn't even realize they were towing ...," muses Frank aloud, but Carmen does not pause to elaborate.

"But there were times when we'd run the stuff right into the dock. One of our boats, and I'll not name her, was really quiet and fast. She was low-structured, like a regular rum-runner, and her engines were all muffled. When her engines were running, you couldn't hear a thing. We run in and unloaded right in the docks. But I only made the one trip on her. I didn't like the skipper."

"Now, with Prohibition repealed down in the States, that ends the business there, don't it?" says Frank.

"It's gettin' tougher down there now, but there's still money to be made along the American coast. I liked the work down there. But here on the Canadian coast it's all work and poor pay. On this coast, the loadings are done offshore from the mother ship to our ship. And it's usually unloaded into dories. Handle it all twice out there, and then deliver it ashore somewhere or other, rowing around half the night with up to fifty kegs in a dory gettin' in as close as possible to a hide. You don't get a whole lot of sleep on a job like that."

"I suppose that sort of story accounts for the type of hide

Sergeant Rennie uncovered," AB offers, who up until this point had contributed little to the conversation. Closing time coming up, thank goodness, he's thinking, with a glance at The Shop's simple alarm clock ticking away the evening on a shelf behind the counter.

"Yes, you got that right," said Carmen. "But it wasn't me that helped fill that hide."

"Look here, gentlemen," says AB, "I'm going to have to put in parking meters, if you're planning to sit around here all night."

* * * * *

Pausing on their way home to light up, Roy says to his neighbour, "Titus, did you know that Letoile and I have had a new neighbour for several months now?"

"Oh yeah, and who's that?"

"She's just a kid, a little girl, a year or so older than our Elaine. Apparently she's been assigned as a ward of the county into the care of Florence and Perry, next door."

"Oh, that should be good for Florence and Perry, seein' as they don't have any children of their own."

"Well, you'd think so, but I'm not so sure."

"Why is that?"

"Well, for one thing, we hardly ever see the child out-doors. Letoile's not even sure the girl gets fed properly. It's like they keep her under lock and key. She's a year or so older than Elaine, but still an' all, you'd think she'd want to come out and play once in a while. It ain't natural."

"Yes, I remember now," Titus says. "Helen told me something about that ... says Florence doesn't allow the girl, what's her name, to come to the parties that Helen organizes for youngsters from time to time on behalf of Rainbow Haven."

"Pauline Zinck."

"Yes, that's it. I suppose she's related to Perry and Florence?"

"I think she might be in some way, a distant relation. There's Zincks all over the place."

"Helen mentioned the girl comes from a broken family in Feltzen South."

"That's it, I remember, Letoile told me she and the father are distant cousins. After the parents separated, their children – and there were three or four of them – were sent to live with new families. Letoile's from Feltzen South. She knew the family and little Pauline before the parents broke up. You probably know young Teeman, he's Pauline's brother ... lives with your brother-in-law Spinny down there in Lower Rose Bay."

"He's well taken care of down there, you can be sure," says Titus.

"I don't know about the others ... one is named Phoebe. But I have to wonder about the little one livin' next door here. Last week your wife had a party going for the children over the hill. I could hear them singing and playing from the back yard here. The wife went over with Elaine."

"Yes, that's the way Helen does it. The parents are invited along too. The idea is that they contribute something toward Rainbow Haven camp – the summer camp for kids, run by *The Halifax Herald*. It's been goin' now for ten years or more. And there's Farmer Smith's column in the *Herald* – the Rainbow Club – that my kids are always talking about. That's a column in the *Herald* by a reporter, Laura Carter, I think her name is. Right now, our daughter is busy drawin' pictures about ghosts and witches and whatnot, to enter into the Halloween contest. And then there's that Uncle Mel character on CHNS who's always goin' on about Rainbow Haven."

"Well, there's nothin' wrong with any of that," says Roy. "Let the kids have some fun. Helps keep 'em out of trouble. I remember the wife sayin' she asked Florence if she would let

Pauline go along over with her and Elaine. And Florence told her no, that it would be too much for Helen's nerves, and it would just make more work for everyone. Imagine that!"

"It don't make no sense," Titus comments. This was not the sort of problem he was used to dealing with. "Our daughter, Carolyn Emily – she's about the same age as Pauline – says she can't understand why Pauline's not allowed to play with her. She says she really wants Pauline as a friend. And there's not much wrong with Helen's nerves. She likes children, and as a teacher she's used to handling dozens of them." With that, the two men part company in front of Titus's house.

Poached Lobster (1937)

According to some mysterious formula devised by the Department of Fisheries and Oceans, the season for lobster fishing in the Maritimes depends on the jurisdiction, that is to say, the locality. You might suspect that lobsters, which on a matter of principle prefer cool water, would govern their whereabouts accordingly. Confounding this hypothesis, a summer season for lobstering has long been in effect on Prince Edward Island – opening in June and closing in August. During this interval, water temperatures in the Northumberland Strait are warmest. It all happily happens for Islanders at the height of the tourist season, when lobster suppers and Anne of the Island festivals are in full swing, and the economy of the place is splendidly positioned to flourish.

On the South Shore of Nova Scotia, the season is open from December 1 to the end of May, not the warmest time of the year to be on the water in an open boat. The big plus for Nova Scotians of course is that South Shore lobsters are far tastier than those of Northumberland Strait where the crustaceans waste a lot of time trying to find their way through all that red mud. More puzzling to the lobstermen of Riverport and District, however, has always been the long and legal practice of P.E.I. fishermen of keeping and selling canners, the small juveniles which haven't had much time to enjoy life – for them, a sad and unfortunate situation.

Annoying too, because to a man, South Shore fishermen must carry in their boats a device, a simple brass caliper known as a lobster measure, in order to measure the distance from the rostrum (beside the eye) to the trailing end of the thorax (body) of the lobster in order to make sure it does not fall in the undersized category – otherwise there could be trouble. Woe betide the South Shore lobsterman who is caught by the authorities smuggling canners ashore for private consumption. All things considered, it's simply not fair.

My uncle Teddy, an accomplished smuggler, was long-practiced in the art. But sure enough, there came a day – it was a Monday in early December just at lunchtime – when he was surprised by two fisheries officers who appeared unannounced at his back door. A sixth sense, inherited no doubt from his mother, instantly alerted Teddy. Clara Augusta Spindler, at work in her tiny pantry making cream puffs, took evasive action. Into her dirty laundry basket went the surprised lobsters, whose nervous shuffling and scratching were thereby totally muffled.

"Sorry to bother you, sir," says the officer, as he is welcomed into the kitchen by Teddy, "but we have reason to believe you have undersized lobsters on the premises."

"That's ridiculous. I just came in from a haul, and I can offer you some fresh hard-shelled beauties from my crate in the harbour if you like. But undersized lobsters … I doubt you'll find any of those in my crate, and certainly not in my house. If you do, I'd like to know about it. Who are you looking for anyway? Are you sure you're at the right place?"

"You are Captain Spindler, I believe?"

"Yes, I am."

"Okay. If you don't mind, we'll just have a look-see."

"Mother, you heard what the officer said – he seems to think we have some undersized lobsters in the house, and they want to have a look around." Then, with a laugh, to the officer, "Do you want to start your search in the pantry?"

"Well, it's a bit of a mess. I'm in the middle of baking as you can plainly see. But come ahead, if you must, just don't knock my cream puffs over. Here, do you want to try one?" says Clara, as she generously offers a panful of cream puffs around.

Predictably, the officers didn't spend a whole lot of time in Clara's pantry. In fact, one of them merely thrust his head in embarrassment across the doorless doorway into Clara's domain and looked around quickly. Fortunately, it never occurred to him to dig into her laundry basket. To complete their inspection, however, the officers insisted on a tour of the Spindlers' cellar. In their experience, cellars generally could be relied upon as the most likely place to uncover cool crawly contraband – but this time it was not to be. Satisfied with their light lunch of cream puffs, the officers moved on, leaving Teddy and his mother slightly older and wiser.

* * * * *

After having briefly considered the pros and cons of lobstering in Nova Scotia (and the seasonal advantage enjoyed by Islanders), conversation in The Shop that evening turned to poaching.

"I don't hold with anyone who poaches from another man's traps." Willy is about to go on, when Frank interrupts.

"Well, neither do I, but Jimmy and his buddy weren't pulling another man's traps. I have to say, though, for the man without a license and who can't outright afford a feed of lobsters, there are lots of different ways of catching 'em. Now whether or not you call it poaching is a matter of opinion."

"What do you mean?" asks Willy. "Scuba divers make a pretty good haul of it sometimes under ideal conditions, and out of season, before the real fishermen get started … I'd call that poaching."

"Scuba divers are a special case all on their own," offers Roy.

"What do you mean by different ways of poaching lobsters, Frank?" Austin asks, his curiosity aroused, like his sudden urge for a good feed of lobster.

"Well, no one's accusin' anybody of poachin'. I'm just sayin' you don't need a regular trap to catch 'em. Scuba divers are pretty good at catchin' lobsters, but they need a lot of expensive gear. Like Roy says, they're kind of a special case. You probably remember how, back in October well before the season opened, fisheries officers caught Jimmy and his pal poachin' off Conrad Island one evening."

"That was all the news for a while there," says Austin.

"Jimmy had rigged up a simple trap out of a length of an old mackerel net. This was weighed down at four corners, and had a ganging leading up to a buoy on the surface. In the middle of the net of course they tied down a mess of fish – skulpins, fish heads, and whatnot."

"That'll do it all right," says Willy, the most experienced shore fisherman among the lot of loafers that evening.

"It worked well," Frank continues. "They had a couple of good hauls and after little more than an hour or so, came ashore in their old punt. Then off home they went along the old shore trail pushing a wheelbarrel full of lobsters. Only unbeknownst to them, Ainsley Fralick, the fisheries officer from Lunenburg, had been keeping pretty close watch on 'em all this while. He and his assistant hid themselves in the long grass beside the track. So here comes old Jimmy pushing along a wheelbarrel load of lobsters.

"Now I don't know if you know Ainsley Fralick, but I do. He is a very big man, and when he rose up suddenly out of the grass beside the track, old Jimmy fainted dead away. He collapsed right into Fralick's arms."

"Hey! And what about his buddy?"

"I was told he made off into the bush. But of course he was rounded up eventually, and he and Jimmy faced the music in court."

"Cost 'em a lot in the end, I'd imagine," offers Willy. "Their boat wouldn't be worth anything much, but the fine would bite."

"I've heard that in the old days, you could catch lobsters at night on a low tide in shallow water. Wade into the water and scoop 'em up, just like that, they was so plentiful. You could always try that trick, Austin."

"Sounds like a hard way to make a living," says Austin, "a lot of work too. I'm not even sure I believe it either. There's got to be easier ways to sneak in a feed of lobsters on the cheap every once in a while. What do you say, Frank?"

"It might be best you get a boat to begin with. Nothing fancy, mind you, just a little rowboat like my boys use for spearing flatties. They catch 'em to sell for lobster bait. With luck, in a boat like that, an' a bit of equipment, you might even be able to spear a lobster or two if you're in the right place. 'Course you could always try scuba diving if you're up to it, or snorkelling, or even better, repair an old trap and set it out with a small marker cork. My boys catch the odd one with a dip net. But that trick calls for two people. Someone's got to maneuver the boat."

"I'll think about it," says Austin.

"The thing is, conditions have to be just right … low tide, no wind, a steady man on the oars, and a dead fish or two on the bottom for bait. You have to have a large dip net, not a round one, but one that's straight across on the far end. And if you're fishing at night, a good head lamp.

"You'd be surprised how well they show up on the bottom – and how quickly they turn up after the bait. They got noses like Alsatians. Even three- and four-pounders play around and hide under rocks and between big rocks in near the shore – makes no difference day or night. Could be they prefer the nighttime. 'Course, the dip net must be a pretty good size, wide-mouthed, with a handle about eight feet long. They're skittish, and you have to come up behind them with it 'cause they swim backwards.

"It takes patience and practice, not to mention time. With me it's mostly been a matter of pure luck. Things look different under water. The angle of your dip net is distorted by the water, making it easy to miss the target which, in the case of a lobster, is more likely than not on the move."

"They always try to escape backwards of course," says Willy. "It's no good pushing the dip net up toward the front end of 'em."

"Sounds like you know all about it," says Frank. "Anyways, it's a fine sport, and when all's said and done, it can't much harm the industry. It's good fun too, if you can spare the time – should be a provincial sport. Why, tourists would pay big money for the privilege of hunting lobsters. You can't call it poaching if they pay for it."

"Frankie, you and I could charge them for showing 'em how it's done. Now, listen up, I'll tell you something you probably won't believe," Willy offers, commanding immediate attention. "Last year I caught a big soaker that way. I was coming in from fishing, about to row ashore in my dory when I spotted a monster on the bottom, on the eel grass, just skullin' along easy like, takin' a little walk. I couldn't believe the size of the thing. But of course, like Frankie said, they look a lot bigger under water. So, over the side went the dip net. And although I didn't catch him in the net – it would have been too small to hold him anyway – he caught hold of the twine just as I was raising it up. Hanging there by a single thread he was, didn't know enough to let go when he had the chance. He only let go as I swung him over the side. Right into the bottom of the boat he fell. And this one I caught in July – hardest kind of shell, and fully packed."

"What did it weigh?"

"I'd say about seven or eight pounds. He was way too big for the pot. And this is where the damn'dest thing happened.

We had to cook him up for supper in two lots, see, body in one pot and pincers in another. Cooked him up that way for all of twenty-five minutes to half an hour – bright red he was. And I'm thinkin' the big claw would make a nice souvenir. Poured off the water and I'm holding the claw in one hand with an oven mitt. So my wife, she says, 'Go on and put your finger in the pincer and see if he'll pinch it.'

"No harm in doing that now, I told her, and to prove it I put my index finger on the tip end of the big pincer. Well, damned if it didn't snap shut on the tip of my finger. It drew blood, you, I'm not makin' this up. I got a witness."

Willy's yarn nevertheless draws a good deal of doubt among his fellow loafers, seeing as none of them had ever before heard of such a thing. "Most likely you hadn't cooked it long enough," Austin offers, an explanation which would have made more sense if Willy had not insisted that the lobster was well-cooked and consumed for supper to everyone's satisfaction.

"And how do you know it was a male lobster?" asks Austin, playing devil's advocate. But to this, Willy makes ready answer.

"Why, the tail of a male is way wider than a female's. An' on the male there's two little boney paddles just behind the body. All the other little paddles they use for swimmin' – there's a special name for 'em ... I forget what it is. The three or four pairs leading back towards the end of the tail are soft and feathery. And of course this one didn't have any eggs."

"Tell me, Willy, was that big one left-handed or right-handed?" asks Frank, who first started the whole discussion. "No, I mean it. I've noticed the crushing pincer can be on either side of a lobster – right or left side. How come? Is it a male and female thing, or is it just a matter of chance?" But to this question no one offers reply.

"Here's somethin' you fellers can try for yourself next time you get hold of a live one."

"What's that?"

"Put it to sleep before you drop it into the boiling water."

"Yeah sure, that way they feel no pain, right? Tell us another one, Willy."

"No, it's easy, you just hold the lobster upright, vertical. Male or female it don't matter, with the pointy end down, touching the table. Hold it there for about a minute, and it goes right still – it don't wiggle at all."

"My youngest boy does that with chickens," says Titus, "except first he puts the chicken's head under its wing, then he holds it there while he swings it back and forth – or 'round and 'round a couple of times, it makes no difference. He calls it hypnotizing a chicken."

"So what happens then?"

"Well, nothin' happens, and that's the whole point. After he puts the chicken back on the ground it don't move at all for the longest time. After a while, it will ever so slowly poke its head out to have a look around. Then it wakes up and takes off. It's the funniest damn thing to watch. Could be this hypnotism thing works with lobsters too."

"I'll maybe believe you about hypnotizing chickens and lobsters," says Austin. "But havin' a cooked lobster – poached or not – nip your finger, why, that's ridiculous."

"Now, here's one for you," says Roy, speaking up from his favourite corner. "You mentioned earlier about lobster eggs, Willy. There's a funny thing about lobster eggs. I've always wondered about this. The eggs, or as some people call it 'the coral,' occurs as clumps inside the body of the lobster, right? But how can that stuff be eggs when, under female lobsters, you see the eggs clear as can be, stuck outside the body, under the tail of the thing?"

"And that roe, or coral, occurs right along with that disgustin' green stuff, inside the guts of the lobster," says Austin.

"Yeah, most people call that green stuff tomalley ... and don't ask me why, 'cause I don't know," says Willy. "But a lot of people eat the tomalley and the coral."

"Some people really like the tomalley," says Titus, "I know my kids eat it like jam, given the chance."

"Disgustin'!" Austin says. "They can't know any better."

"Humpf!" Titus growls, scowling at Austin, fair enough warning of foul weather in the offing.

"Do chickens lay eggs?" asks Frank.

"Yeah, they do," says Austin, "but they don't go 'round with them stuck under their tails. Lobsters can't have eggs in both places, inside of 'em and outside as well, under their tails."

"Willy, you'll have to explain that to us if you can," says Frank.

"Not sure I can," Willy answers. "But I know Fisheries tells us we have to release what are called 'seed lobsters' or 'berried lobsters.' These are the ones – female of course – with bunches of tiny round things that look like little half-ripe huckleberries under their tails. And they can have them any time of the year at all, summer or winter, makes no difference. You figure it out from there."

"So what comes first, the coral or the seed? It's the chicken and the egg thing all over again," says Austin.

"That I don't know. You might have to take up scuba diving to find out how lobsters really get things done," Frank advises Willy.

"And while you're at it check up on their brains," says Austin. "I heard tell a lobster's brain is somewhere just behind the eyeballs."

"I thought it was under the tail," says Willy.

"More questions than answers tonight," says AB, as he commences to close up shop. "More research is clearly needed. Someone should start a survey."

"There's another job for you, Willy," says Frank.

Close to Home (October 1940)

As they make their way to The Shop that evening, Roy mentions to his neighbour, "Did I tell you we lost our little neighbour a short while ago?"

'What do you mean?" asks Titus. "I didn't hear of anybody dyin' recently around here."

"No one died, Titus. I'm talking about Pauline Zinck, the little girl Florence and Perry took in as a ward of the county. She's about ten now, and for some reason or other, after almost five years with Florence and Perry, she's been moved down to Lower Rose Bay to live with Bernard and Mabel Risser."

"They have a daughter of their own, don't they?"

"Yes, they do, a young one, and that's a good thing. It'll be good for Pauline to be in a real home for a change. Florence and Perry don't understand the first thing about kids. Letoile says the child's been half-starved livin' with them. I'm not even sure they know where children come from."

"G'way."

"No, I mean it. I heard a story about one young married couple who believed a woman gets pregnant through her belly button. The story goes the young fella pretty well wore hisself out testing that theory."

"I imagine his wife was worn a bit thin too."

"Rissers keep a store, so there's people comin' and goin' all the time. The girl will have more of a normal life there than she'd ever have stayin' on with Florence and Perry. She's had a rough time of it with them two. Letoile tells me that after her parents left her, and each other, she was taken in by a good family up back of Bridgewater, but the police came lookin' for the girl. Seems they had their orders, I guess, and that was to place Pauline in a home chosen by the county. I'm not sure how it works, but when they came 'round to the home in Bridgewater, those kind people hid her away so they couldn't find her. Next thing, the police went to the school, forced her out, and gave her into to Florence and Perry. It's not a pretty story. Things went from bad to worse for a time. Thank goodness she's found a safe haven now. Rissers treat her like family."

"You got to wonder what they're thinkin'," Titus muses, though he was not about to press the inquiry, adding only, "Anyways, like you, I reckon it's turned out for the best."

It can hardly be expected that either man could properly appreciate Pauline's life story. Suffice to say, perhaps the authorities of the day, police included, were not the most charitably minded. The fact remains, however, a good portion of Pauline's early life was marked by nightmares, clinging like burrs to her memory.

* * * * *

"That's gettin' close to home," Frank was saying to AB as the men entered The Shop.

"What's gettin' close? Is it safe to come in here?" asks Roy.

"Oh, we was just talkin' 'bout the *Bras d'Or*, she's that minesweeper disappeared in the Gulf of St Lawrence earlier this week. Probably lost with all hands."

"It was on the news a night or so ago," says AB. "Orginally built as a trawler, *Bras d'Or* served as a lightship until she was made over into a minesweeper early in the war. A lot of our ships were made into minesweepers and crewed by local fishermen. They all carry the stamp HMT – His Majesty's Trawler."

"Any local men on her, do you know?" Titus asks.

"Well, we all know Tommy Conrad," says AB.

"That we do, but he's at home."

"He lives just down the hill a ways from me, and it's his son – Walter was captain of the *Bras d'Or.*"

"Oh my."

"Damned shame if she's sunk," mutters Titus. "But she could still show up." A sentiment shared by everyone, though followed by a silence offered as it were in tribute to lives possibly lost.

"Tommy and Grace have two boys, don't they?" asks Roy.

"Yes," AB answers, "Gordon and Walter. Still, it'd be a mighty hard blow."

"Good evening to you, gentlemen," says the lean but sprightly old fellow who enters The Shop at that moment.

"Evenin', doctor," comes the general response. Dr. Geoffrey Barss is the well-respected medical authority in the district.

"I thought to drop by and pick up some of your excellent cheese before you close," he says to AB, who prepares to uncover the glass case containing the remaining portion of his cheese wheel.

"Afraid it's getting a little green around the edges, Dr. Barss. Would you prefer I trim it a bit?"

"No, I'll take it as is – not fit to eat otherwise," says the doctor.

"Fancy him, of all people, preferring moldy cheese," says Roy, to no one in particular, shortly after the doctor takes leave of the company.

"Could be he knows something we don't," offers Titus.

"You'll find no one to argue with that," says AB.

"I got a lot of respect for him. He served on the Western Front during the war. His wife, Eda Claire, went overseas with him as a nursing sister, stationed in France. She's from New-foundland originally."

"You know his son Allison is in the air force, don't you?" says AB.

"I'd sooner be in the air than on the ground in any war," says Austin.

"Was it him in that yellow plane that flew over yesterday afternoon? It was so low I thought it might hit the church stee-ple," says Frank. "Whoever it was waggled his wings too, did you notice?"

"That was Lowell Mossman. Like the doctor's son, he joined the RCAF early on in the war. But Allison is overseas now, I believe," says AB. "Three or four local boys have joined the air force. There's Clifford Niford for one, and Robbie Mosh-er's boy, Keith, from down in Lower LaHave, is another."

"Somebody told me that plane was a Mosquito," says Frank.

"A what? A Mosquito? You're kidding!" says Austin.

"No, hold on, that plane was a Harvard Trainer," AB ex-plains, "a single-engine job, likely flying out of Debert. But, Austin, there is a plane known as a Mosquito; in fact, there are two types of Mosquito aircraft. One's the de Havilland Mosqui-to. It's a fighter. The other is the Pathfinder, a bomber. Both of them are two-seaters."

"How come you know so much?" asks Austin.

"AB's in the citizen's Aircraft Detection Corps," says Frank. "He helps keep tabs on what's going on around here, just in case the Germans show up. So you better behave yourself."

"What's that? I never heard of that. Is that true, AB?" asks Austin.

"Yes. The Aircraft Detection Corps was set up last year, right across Canada. It's run by volunteers. The idea is to know who's using our air space. We report, too, on any sightings of U-Boats off the coast. We have seaplanes – Catalinas and Can-sos – that help out on coastal patrols. But they're backed up by bombers, including the Pathfinder. U-Boats are easier to see from the air than from a ship."

"See them from a ship, and it's probably too late," says Titus.

"So you think Lowell wasn't just showing off for the girls?" says Frank. "He's quite a daredevil, you know. When he's home he's usually tearing around the place on his motorcycle. He's always got one girl or another in his sidecar."

"Well, you can be sure there was no girl in the plane with him."

"Somebody was sayin' the other day they use whales for target practice," says Austin.

"I doubt it. Who told you that anyway?" asks AB. "But I suppose mistakes can happen. Only a week ago, a large dead whale washed ashore down off Cape Sable Island. Observers phoned in about it, thinking it was a U-Boat surfaced close to shore."

"It could have been hit by a passing ship too. That happens sometimes," says Frank. "Why, I remember ..." He was about to continue when a strange yelling sounded from outside The Shop.

"Oh, that'll be Carmen Creaser. He's a Hank Snow fan, just like me, didn't you know?" says Frank. "I hope you like yodelling."

> *Ah de oh ley de oh!*
> *Oh de ley de oh, oh, oh!*
> *There is the sweetest girl I know,*
> *Her heart is beating true.*
> *And when the golden sunset glows,*
> *I'll yodel back to you.*

"Oh, so that's what the racket is all about ... you must be in love again," Frank says, as Carmen bursts in the door.

"Can't beat the Yodelling Ranger at that!" says Carmen. "That, an' singin' and tap dancin'."

"I like Wilf Carter better than Hank Snow," says Frank.

"Hank Snow is from down near Liverpool, Liverpool or Brooklyn, I think," says Roy. "An' you got to give the man his due, considerin' how well he's been makin' his way. I sailed with him once, on the *Grace Boehner* with Lapene Crouse. We called him Jack. It was his first trip – played his harmonica and guitar on board. He could sing too. Nice fella."

"Still is!" says Carmen. "And tonight he's playing at Molega. He's a rising star. I'm going up. Anybody want to come with?"

"What makes you so sure he's gonna show up?" asks Amos. "Wasn't he supposed to come to Riverport a while back, set to play in the IOOF hall? He usually stays in the Myrtle Hotel."

"You should know," says Carmen. "He was hot after courtin' your girl, Marion, there for a while."

"Oh, that was years ago. We're married now."

"When did you and Marion get married anyway?" asks Roy.

"December 28, 1936."

"Any kids yet?"

"No, we're workin' on it."

"You know, Amos, some of the women, my wife Thursa for one, they're still wondering how come Marion wore a red velvet dress. She says it was the talk of the community at the time. I know it's ridiculous, but it's got me curious too. Was there some particular reason for the red dress?"

"That I don't know. Women are funny. Can't say as I can answer that question. You'll have to ask Marion."

"She was just such hot stuff, Roy, that would explain the dress," says Carmen, who, with scarcely a pause, continues his story about Hank Snow's escapade. "I remember there was one time Hank Snow set out for Riverport, but never did make it. They say he got into the sauce and hit a tree on the way out of Halifax."

"He probably phoned ahead and cancelled that time," says Roy, offering a belated excuse for Hank.

"You better hope he makes it to Molega tonight, Carmen, else you're wastin' gas. It'll be a long drive for nothin'. You can hear him on CHNS tomorrow mornin', if you get up early enough," says Roy. "That's if he makes it back to Halifax tonight."

"It won't be for nothing. He'll be there, don't worry. I'll chance it. Hey there, young fella, how's it goin'?" said Carmen to the teenager, Douglas Himmelman, who entered the store just then.

"Oh pretty good. I'm set for goin' fishin' with my father on the *Bessemer*. He said he'd take me on his next trip to the Banks."

"Well, that's good. Too bad you were born too late – missed out on the high times during rum-running," says Carmen.

"Can't turn back the clock, but I did get a bit of time in."

"What do you mean? How would you manage that?"

"Well, it hardly counts as rum-runnin', but I remember when Jimmy Himmelman, a buddy of mine and I, stood watch one night on the *Mudathalapadu* when she was in port just before making her last trip. I think we got two dollars a night for standing watch. That allowed all the crew to take off – we loved that. There was lots of good food to eat aboard her, see."

"The *Muddythelapswho* ... that's a funny name," says Austin.

"Rum-runners didn't worry much about names," Carmen explains. "Boats of the Banana Fleet all looked pretty much the same. We usually changed the name board a couple of times after leaving port to make it difficult for the police and Coast Guard to identify and track us. Make it harder for 'em."

"That's so," says Frank, "but who came up with all of those crazy names? I heard of one called *Etchipotchi*, and then there was the *Popacatapult* – only she got caught – and ..."

"Sound like Mi'kmaq names," Austin interrupts Frank as he is about to elaborate.

"Could be," says Titus.

"I heard you got into some trouble over that, Doug," Frank comments.

"How'd you know that?"

"Oh, I had friends in the business around about that time."

"Well, it's no great secret, but yeah, we messed up in the engine room. There was a furnace in there and we put a can of spaghetti on top of it without taking the cover off. It exploded and made quite a mess of things. Robert Cook was the fellow who rang my bell, because he was the engineer – he was the one who likely told you the story."

"Yeah, he was," says Frank.

"He wasn't very happy with it, having to clean spaghetti off the engine."

"I don't imagine he was," says Carmen. "But hey, look 'a here, I gotta go. Anybody comin' with me? Douglas? You still goin' with Sylvia Mosher? We can go pick her up and take her along with, if you like. There's still time."

"No, I can't go. My money's all spent, and Sylvia's got the flu."

"No? Well, I'm off. See you later." With that, and grabbing his package of pop and cigarettes, Carmen is out the door with a bang.

"Did he say Sylvia Mosher is your girlfriend, Douglas?" asks Roy in astonishment.

"We're just good friends really. We went to school together in Lunenburg after my parents moved from here to town. Her father was lost at sea off Sable in 1926. His house came up for sale and my father, he bought it and we moved to Lunenburg. Our place is out there near Rous's Brook, four or five houses down. There's two houses exactly alike side by side; the other one belongs to Captain Leo Corkum. But I know what you're gettin' at. Yes, Sylvia is Captain John Mosher's daughter. Nice girl. He named his ship after her."

"Lost in the August gale of '26. All twenty-five hands, gone," Roy says to himself, recalling an earlier trauma.

"It's a small world we're in," says Douglas.

"That Carmen sure is full of himself. Bit of a blowhard, ain't he? He can't still be rum-running, can he?" says Austin.

"Sounds like it ... who knows? All piss and vinegar." This from Amos, to no one in particular.

The Younger Generation (October 1944)

Autumn brought a familiar change to the communities of Riverport and District. Most fishermen were home enjoying a well-deserved break from their trade. Fish prices had never been better, thanks to the stupendous war effort going on. At home, domestic preparations prior to winter were underway – cutting and hauling next year's supply of wood, sawing, chopping, and piling it so it would dry in good time and order. Numerous were the jobs engendered by growing families occupying multi-generational old homes.

In the nearby town of Lunenburg, shipyards were humming as Smith and Rhuland continued building sailing ships and launched the *Sherman Zwicker*, its largest schooner ever. Dozens of corvettes, minesweepers, and frigates were undergoing refitting at the Lunenburg Foundry. Construction of Camp Norway was completed along Tannery Road and was taken over by the Norwegian Navy as a naval training station. Germany invaded Norway in the spring of 1940; providentially, nearly the full complement of ships of Norway's merchant marine was at sea. At the time, the small nation of Norway had the third largest ocean-going merchant fleet in the world.

Across the world's oceans those ships received conflicting sailing instructions. From the Nazis' Quisling puppet government: "Return to port as soon as possible!" But King Olav V's counter order "Proceed immediately to allied ports!" was the one obeyed by every Norwegian ship.

Seven factory ships and twenty-two whalers, which had been whaling in Antarctic waters, arrived in Halifax in 1940 with more than two thousand men on board. Subsequently, Norway was allowed to establish Camp Norway in Lunenburg in order to accommodate eight hundred whalers. Their flag was raised in the camp for the first time on November 29, 1940. Before long, the Norwegian Navy turned it into a naval training station, and in both 1941 and 1942, Crown Prince Olav and Crown Princess Martha were welcomed as visitors to the town.

Local events to support the war effort took place in rural Nova Scotian communities. Weeks after the event was held in early fall, people continued to talk about the success of a concert and sale held by the children of Rose Bay for The Queen's Canadian Fund for Air Raid victims in Great Britain, and for Rainbow Haven.

In her report to Farmer Smith's column in *The Halifax Herald*, twelve-year-old Carolyn Emily writes that "Mr. John Risser gave us the use of his hall, which Mr. Murray Ritcey kindly wired for the occasion. Miss Nellie Colp, Mrs. Flossie Conrad, Mrs. Perry Zinck, Mrs. Ronald Mossman, Misses Lorna Conrad and Lois Knock, Mrs. Leroy Deal, Mrs. Albert Mossman, mother (Helen Titus) and Russel Zinck, helped in the various sellings etc., and the children who took part were: Jean Backman, Shirley Conrad, Virginia Wamboldt, George Mossman, Billy and Donald Himmelman, Pauline Zinck, Phyllis Dodge, Dorothy Deal, Doris Himmelman, Doris Schrader, Winnie Wentzell, Greta Wamboldt, Margaret Jean Lohnes, Shirley Mossman, Elaine Deal, Marguerite Cook, Joan Winters, Burlington Deal, Bobby Zinck, Sylvia Deal, Ray Zinck, Marina Zinck, Betty Knock, Sylvia Conrad, Eileen Meisner, Pauline Meisner, Mona Conrad,

Frank Oxner, Evelyn Mossman, Douglas Romkey, Harry Conrad, and Bobby Mossman."

Farmer Smith of Rainbow Haven duly praised the "little Rainbows" for their splendid work, noting that a similar concert was being organized by another group of "little people" at Pentz, a small community west of Bridgewater. She gratefully acknowledged that the total sum (twenty-seven dollars) realized by the Rose Bay concert – the sale of admission tickets (at ten cents each), tickets sold (two dollars) on a decorated cake, tickets sold (five dollars) on a quilt pieced together by Carolyn Emily's mother, and the purchase of various mothers-made fancy work, homemade candy, and "grabs" – exceeded by nearly ten dollars the sum earned by the same group of children at their concert held the year previous (a sum equivalent to approximately $395 today). Not bad, all things considered.

By late October, the fall colours were shorn from sparse hardwood stands, and the yellowing needles of tamarack (larch) slightly relieved an otherwise blanketing background of spruce green in the countryside. The grey dirt road continued to snake its way southward toward Lower Rose Bay and the two Kingsburgs. Beside The Shop in Upper Rose Bay, Arthurs Brook burbled nonchalantly non-stop over a final patch of gravel before being swallowed up in the muskrat-infested salt marsh corralled by Rose Bay Beach. Frank Zinck's three sons – Robert (Bobby), Ray, and Allison – faithfully trapped the rodents.

Little Allison is at the counter asking for candy, money gripped tightly in hand. "How much can I get for ten cents?" he asks AB who, with ready smile, looks the child over carefully.

"I could sell you six pieces for ten cents. But you really don't need all that. How's about I give you half as much?"

"No, I think I'd like six pieces."

"All right then," says AB, as he slowly counts out the six pieces of penny candy into a small paper bag and passes them to Allison. "Here you are."

"Smart little fella you have there, Frank," says Roy, as Frank advises the little fellow to get on home. Allison deftly squeezes out of the door past a new arrival, William Leary. Frank, Willy, Roy, and Titus are already comfortably ensconced along the south wall of The Shop.

"He's just a little nixnutz – he should be home in bed by this time," says Frank. "Talk about bein' smart, do you know what those boys have been up to on your brook, Arthur?"

"Well, it's not my brook, you know. The old maps show it as Hirtle Brook. But which boys, and what have they been up to?"

"I heard Frank's boy, Bobby, the oldest one, has been givin' boxing lessons to Titus's boy," says Austin.

"Oh, is that so? George hasn't said anythin' about that," Titus replies.

"Bobby's a good bit taller than George, and I expect he's got a longer reach too," Austin adds. "I doubt he'd last long up against Bobby."

"Wearing glasses wouldn't help him much either," says AB.

"You're right there," says Frank. "Anyways, I was told he only lasted one round, so couldn't a' been much damage done. But what I really set out to tell Titus about has nothing to do with boxing."

"Frank must be thinkin' about the dam some boys were workin' on a ways downstream from the culvert. Boys are always up to somethin' or other. Kids dam off little streams just for the fun of it," says Willy.

"Don't know about boys damming off streams," says Austin, "but the girls around here spend a lot of their time playing tennis on the court up by the Lutheran Church. That's where the older boys can be found most of the time too, for that matter."

"It's only natural," says AB.

"Never had much time for that myself," says Titus. "Don't know where my childhood went."

"That's only part of it," says Frank, ignoring Titus's off-hand remark. "Bobby and young Harry Conrad, across the road from us, they built that dam. It was 'round about the time of the Sunday school picnic, and no one paid much attention to them at first. Like you say, boys are always up to something or other. The next thing we knew, they rigged up a water wheel in the dam. The thing is powered by water running over the dam as the tide comes in."

"Now, they're neither of 'em teenagers yet, and be damned – excuse the language, AB – they're powering electricity from an old car generator with a switch on to it, all hooked up to the water wheel set in the dam. Night before last they had the place lit up like a Christmas tree. Lights all 'round the dam. Lots of neighbours come by to see it in operation. I think Harry is the brains behind it. He reads every issue of *Popular Mechanics* he can get his hands on. Why, the two of 'em even rigged up a telephone line. I discovered that a week or so ago. Bobby had bits and pieces of gear spread all over his bed and a thread o' wire run out of his bedroom window across the highway to Harry's room on the other side. That way they could talk to each other after they went to bed in the evening."

"They should have no trouble gettin' jobs ashore!" exclaims Austin.

"Harry will make a good engineer. But I'm not so sure about Bobby," says Frank.

"I can't say about your boy, Frank," says Titus, "or mine either. But Reverend Pace has pretty well convinced George to go into the ministry. Helen's pleased as Punch of course, and I'm not altogether disappointed. George is still pretty young, and all that could change in time. As for Bobby, you told me yourself he was thinkin' about the ministry. You can't be a minister and an engineer both. But at least they shouldn't end up havin' to go to sea like us."

"Well, it could turn out they'll join the ministry. Bobby talks about it every once in a while, but I doubt very much if anything will ever come of it. Fact is, I don't believe either one of 'em is cut out for preachin'. If anything, they're doin' a good job leadin' each other astray."

"Why do you say that?" asks Titus in growing alarm.

"I don't suppose you heard what they were up to last Sunday during the service? I'm surprised your wife didn't mention it to you."

'No, I didn't hear. I was at sea. What happened anyway? Tell me," Titus urges.

"Well, most of the singin' and prayin' and the like was done with, and Reverend Pace, he was more 'n halfways launched into his sermon. All the while them two boys was carrying on in a pew at the back of the church."

"What were they doin'?"

"Look a here, you probably ain't gonna believe this, Titus, but it's true. They were playing checkers."

"Checkers!"

"Yes, Chinese checkers, and they weren't schusseling around, they were bein' pretty quiet about it. That is, they were until ..."

"Chinese checkers? I don't believe it!" Titus interrupts, barely suppressing his growing storm of indignation.

"Yes, Chinese checkers. They even brought the board to church. Trouble was, a couple of the checkers – they're marbles of course – got away from 'em and begun rollin' slowly down the side of the aisle, one after the other on the wooden floor. Now that dry old wood doesn't do much to mask the noise. Those marbles just rolled along, takin' their time – of course that made everyone sit straight up an' pay attention. All the way down to the front of the church they rolled. And that's where the real racket began. You know what's there in front of the communion stand, don't you?"

By this time, there were smiles breaking out all around, as many of the loafers imagined themselves as boys once again, when they too could afford to be so foolish.

"No, what?" asks Titus, by this time red-faced, though slowly recovering as he noticed the smiles building all around him. Truth be known, attending church was by no means his favourite activity either. He much preferred to stay at home on Sundays, to make sure dinner was ready for all the returning church-goers in his family – at least that's what he told us.

"There's a hot air register on the floor in front of the communion table, see, and the marbles dropped one after the other ... *dingle, dingle, dingle,* then ... *clink, clink, clinkity-clink,* around each corner as they made their way down into the bowels of the furnace room. People couldn't figure out what was going on at first, and there were some odd looks all 'round. I have to say, though, the Reverend took it well. I suppose he must ha' been thinking, 'Boys will be boys.' But it might do to at least have a word with your oldest to make sure it don't happen again. We shouldn't be too hard on 'em, though – they're barely teenagers after all. But like I say, they'll have to do some serious repentin' if they plan to go into the ministry."

"That I will," says Titus, somewhat sobered by this revelation.

* * * * *

"That brook of yours is good for a lot of things besides fishing," says Willy. "Bernie Deal was down cleaning entrails for casings for puddings and sausages after killing one of his pigs last week."

"Yes, it's real handy for that sort of thing. My father, Rufus, does that almost every year," says AB.

"There was quite a gathering up on Bernie's Hill last Wednesday morning when I went up there to help out," says Frank. "My boys took off at recess from the school. So did most all of 'em from the upper grades, including some girls. It's good for the boys to learn how things work, but I don't know about the girls. Their teacher, Miss Pentz, didn't have much choice, I suppose. She's a good-looking girl. I think Bobby's in love with her. All the boys are. Anyway, most of 'em took off from school in the morning.

"After Lennox stunned the pig with a mallet, Lowell Mossman killed it with a shot to the head. Then, after the guts were removed, the kids crowded 'round after the body was dumped into the trough and had boiling water poured all over it – the usual thing. Some of the bigger boys helped scrape hair off it with sharp knives, but the men did most of the work. I understand you're smoking some of the hams and the bacon, over at your place, aren't you, Roy?"

"Yeah, I am."

"You know, I was surprised Bernie keeps all of the waste cuts and even some of the guts," says Frank. "He tells me he feeds it to his other pigs. I guess there's no real harm in that, but it does seem a bit rough and unusual. I know pigs will eat just about anything, especially if they're hungry enough."

"Well, Bernie's a bit rough and unusual himself," says Willy, with the certainty that Roy won't disagree with this assessment of his brother. "But there's no doubt his pigs ought to make pretty good bacon."

"Hmm … bacon-fed pigs! Yum!" Austin exclaims, clapping his hands on his knees.

"You can say what you like, but the best sausages and puddings around are made by old Ralph Acker over in First South," says Roy. "I've asked him for his recipe, but he won't tell me or anyone else. He keeps it to himself. He's a worker too, second in a large family. Twenty-one kids, if you can believe it, and every one of 'em lived to tell the tale – every last one of 'em. Did you ever hear the like? He's got a job on the CNR railway. He's one of two men who operate the jitney what runs between Lunenburg and Mahone Bay. Four round trips they make, every day of the week except Sundays. He's been workin' there since it started up, in 1937, I believe it was."

"Is he the conductor or the engineer?"

"I'm not sure. But it only takes two men to run a jitney … it's a self-propelled railcar," says Frank. "In fact, there's not even a diesel engine on that rig. It's all powered by a bunch of batteries under the floor. A traction motor runs the wheels. I've been on it once or twice. Each day the batteries get charged overnight in Lunenburg, and away they go next day. It's a real handy rig for gettin' around in."

"Good job if you can get it," says Willy, who can't help comparing work on a self-propelled railcar to his busy round of shore fishing.

"That poor Mrs. Acker … Ellen, isn't it," says Roy. "You gotta wonder how that woman manages, lookin' after so many kids … most all of 'em girls, not to mention givin' birth to 'em, one after the other."

"Yeah, every nine months and fifteen minutes …," says Willy.

"There must ha' been a little somethin' extra in some of them sausages," says Frank.

AB had gone quiet, a sure sign of his disapproval of such rude talk. But Roy misses the "joke," and instead simply points out, "Of course the older ones would be helpin' out with the younger ones. I'd imagine the family always kept a few pigs. But in my family, we never let girls watch anything as gross as slaughtering an animal. It's different with boys. In a way, I suppose it doesn't really matter when you come right down to it. The boys will supply the girls with all the gory details afterwards anyways, including the sounds,"

"Yeah, they're good at that," adds Frank.

"You could say I've got some pretty wild relatives up there on the hill," says Roy. "But you know, some of 'em is wilder than others. Burlington, the boy – Bubba – he gets into trouble all the time. It's like he goes lookin' for it. He's a regular rapscallion. And Dorothy, the youngest girl, is definitely on the wild side. I wish 'em well, but disciplining that crowd is none of my business. It's beyond my helpin'. Bernard takes no advice from me."

Sea Turtles and U-Boats (September 1945)

"Helen told me your wife had a fall some time ago. How's she doin'?" Titus asks Roy as they walk up to The Shop.

"Letoile's better now, but still on the mend. I missed the last trip. Someone must look after the animals, and the garden, and whatnot. But I might go halibutin' with Rollie before the end of the month. How's 'bout you?"

"I have to say, the summer trip wasn't very good. But I'm goin' to take some time off to paint the house. I've let it go too long already. My oldest boy is big enough to help out a bit now."

"Yeah, he's fast growin' up. He was tellin' me just the other day how much fun he had this summer at the Sunday school picnic over at The Ovens. He said that Oscar Young – he owns the place you know – he said Oscar showed him and some other kids how to pan for gold. That's pretty good of him, wouldn't you say? It's not like the man has nothin' else to do. He's made all them trails and signs, put up a couple of cabins for tourists, an' he's built a small chapel in the woods."

"Yeah, Oscar does a good job of keepin' things goin' over there. The Lutherans have their own church picnic over on Spindlers Beach in Feltzen South, don't they?"

"Some years we have it there, and other times over at the Ovens. Either way, the kids love it. A couple dozen of 'em will pile into the back of Kermit Himmelman's big truck, and off they go. It's the next best thing to Christmas for them. Letoile took Elaine along with her. They left me home."

'Well, George didn't find any gold ... or if he did, he didn't give me any," says Titus. "Oscar gets a few ounces off Cunard Beach every year or so, at least during summer, using some sort of rig he's made up ... a rocker, I think he calls it."

"You're lucky you don't have a farm to look after."

"Just a few chickens. They mostly look after themselves."

"Pauline Zinck's been helpin' out Letoile with the house-work. You remember Pauline, don't you?"

"She's the little girl used to stay with Florence and Perry, isn't she?" says Titus.

"Yeah, but she's not so little any more. She works at Rissers' store, and takes care of the post office some days, but she wants to get a steady paying job. Letoile says she does a lot of babysitting for Dr. Smith, the veterinarian up in Bridgewater. That gets her out and around some – and that's good. He keeps a horse for his kids. Guess she feels she should be doin' more and makin' her own way. And who can blame her, knowin' what she's had to put up with in her young life."

* * * * *

In The Shop that evening, the topic of discussion ranges from turtles to U-Boats. For starters, everyone in the community knew all about sea turtles – or thought they did – for hadn't they seen one iced and on show in the main pavilion every year since the Lunenburg Fisheries Exhibition began? Some adventurers were even familiar with small woodland turtles present in lakes of the district, or with the tiny turtles their children kept as pets in small homemade aquariums.

"Yes," says AB. "Carrie tells me they got a big one on display again this year, all of five or six hundred pounds. She spent the better part of a day there with our youngest, Margaret Jean. They took a couple of rides on Bill Lynch's merry-go-round. Our girl's still talking about the turtle."

"They come pretty big, don't they," Frank mutters, more a statement to himself than a question.

"A leatherback, that's what they're called, leatherback turtles. You see 'em from time to time off the coast hereabouts. But I'm told they range all over the world," offers Willy.

"Margaret Jean, she wants to know what happens to the turtle after the exhibition. I wasn't sure what to tell her. Is it good eating, she asked, or does it get thrown out? I never heard of anyone around here eating turtles, but could be they do. Does anybody know?"

"Well, I don't think you should tell her," says Titus. "It's probably best she doesn't know. All of the fish left over after the exhibition – sunfish, leatherback turtles, sharks, what have you, gets trucked out to National Sea Products at Battery Point and turned into fish meal."

"Ah," AB groans as he hears this. "I was half-afraid to ask. What a shame. I can't tell her that."

"Oh, there's lots of 'em around. You see them every year out in Hartling Bay. I saw one this summer off Cross Island," says Willy.

"Carmen was in here earlier talking about Cross Island," says Roy.

"Oh, and what was he on about this time?"

"He was raving about the Cross Island Hillbillies. Said they were playing in Lunenburg during the exhibition, and he was hoping they'd have another show soon again. I've heard they're pretty good."

"Well, good for Carmen. He seems to have lots of money. Easy come, easy go. But they say the Hillbillies know how to play. Some guy by the name of Harry Hibbs is leader of the group."

"Didn't know there were any musicians on Cross Island. Is Hibbs from the island, do you know?" Roy asks.

"Not sure ... but I know the big attraction a week or so before the exhibition was down on the waterfront in Lunenburg," says Frank. "They brought in a captured U-Boat. Our Canadian frigate *Joliette* escorted her into Lunenburg. I saw the thing come into the harbour past Battery Light – made the hair stand right up on the back of my neck. According to the *Progress-Enterprise*, it was U-Boat 889, one of several that surrendered back in May."

"I went in to see her too ... late afternoon ... a frightening sight even though it was roped to the dock," says Willy.

"The first one I ever saw was on the Banks back during World War I. It scared the bejasus out of us. Another vessel – the *Elsie Porter* – was there fishin' not that far from us. But as soon as our captain saw the sub break surface, he clapped on all sail. Captain Eisenhauer's crew wasn't as lucky. Most of their dories was still out. They had a long row to shore."

"Germans sank their ship?"

"Scuttled her, done her in one way or another, I'm not sure how."

"There'll be huge reparations called for in this war – far bigger even than in the first one, I expect," says Titus.

"At the end of World War I, annual payment to the British Empire amounted to over six hundred million dollars," AB says. "How long this went on for, I can't rightly say. German money wasn't worth very much."

"I don't believe the Germans ever got around to paying the money out," says Titus. "But I know for a fact many people put in claims. My cousin Forman, for one I know, put in a small claim, and my father-in-law, old John Spindler, Dan Romkey's another, and there's the fish buyer, Fraser Gray, put in a big claim. Why, there's got to be dozens of families due reparation money around here – the captains whose ships were sunk by U-Boats, and the fishermen who had shares in schooners. I wouldn't put it past our own government holdin' it back. They could have received the money from England but for some reason or other has been holdin' out makin' the payouts."

"That could easy be," says Frank.

"Didn't you put in a claim, Titus, for what all them war mongrels put you through in the Great War?" Austin asks.

"No, but they nearly did me in."

"Close don't count."

"I've seen some of them German reparation coupons from the first war myself," Willy speaks up, fearing more of Austin's foolish comments. "A cousin of mine down in Lower Kingsburg has several of 'em, but last I heard he hadn't even tried to cash 'em in. Like AB says, they're probably not worth anythin'. They look like Canada Savings Bonds except they got German writin' all over 'em, and are made out in marks."

"If they're made out in marks, they're not worth a whole lot now anyhow."

"Some people, including authorities who ought to know better, suggest those coupons are certificates bought by people in Lunenburg County in order to support the German war effort. Did you ever hear of anything so ridiculous?"

AB says, "If any of you are waitin' around for reparation from this latest war, don't hold your breath 'cause it could be a while. As I understand it, after the Treaty of Versailles in 1919, the Germans only ever paid up a small part of the claims. Far as I know, the issue has not been resolved, even for the First World War."

"It's hard to even imagine the amount of money spent on war, never mind the loss of life," says Roy.

"The Germans had over a thousand submarines during this latest war. We know the damage they've done. It will be even worse than the First World War if they ever get around to settlin' up the claims. I doubt it will ever happen, even after the smoke clears," AB adds.

"Good thing a U-Boat never made it into Bedford Basin," says Willy. "With all them ships packed close together there would ha' been a real mess. The sub wouldn't even have to bother to aim … just keep pullin' the trigger on their torpedo tubes."

"It don't bear thinkin' about," says Frank. "But you know somethin' … we can make a pretty good mess of things all by ourselves without even half-thinkin' about it. Look at that explosion a month ago in the Bedford Magazine. Could easily ha' been a repeat of the 1917 explosion. Does anyone know how that all started, AB?"

"I understand it began with a barge catching fire beside the dock," AB explains. "There was a lot of ammunition piled on the dock for transfer to several RCN ships. Those ships were being readied for the Pacific theatre. The explosions began when the fire spread to the dock itself. There was no U-Boat involved. But it could have been a lot worse."

"I went to Lunenburg to see that U-Boat close up," Willy put in. "People were allowed on board, you know, to look at her insides. I saw you with your daughter Margaret Jean. And Titus, I seen your young feller goin' down the hatch. Some women even went down inside of her, completely open to the public she was. More than fifty men was needed to operate the thing. Packed in like sardines, they must ha' been. It's supposed to be one of the latest models, outfitted with a snorkel, whatever that is."

"U-889 is a model IXC/40, one of the latest models. But there's nothing particularly new about the snorkel. It's been around a long time."

"The snorkel's a breathing pipe that pokes out up on the surface of the water, isn't it," says Frank, "so's to give the men inside fresh air to breath when the sub is submerged."

"One of the main purposes of the snorkel is to take air to the diesel engines in order to recharge them from time to time," AB explains. "With the snorkel the sub doesn't have to surface to recharge its batteries. It just stays at periscope depth, so it's not easily seen. The snorkel folds down horizontal when it's not needed. They say it's not a perfect solution because water often gets into it during stormy weather and … you can imagine the trouble that would cause. This sub was outfitted with radar and radio to help it locate distant targets. New acoustic torpedoes too, which seek out targets provided by the engine noise made by ships."

"How come you know so much about this?" asks Willy, astonished to discover how much this storekeeper knows.

"AB keeps up to date on all this stuff," says Titus, "didn't you know? We talked about this before. AB's with the Aircraft Detection Corps, the ADC."

"Yes, I've been with the ADC since the mid-1940s when it was formed. Volunteers were recruited from all across Canada. There's over two and a half thousand observation posts. Ours is one of them."

"Did you get special training for this?" asks Willy.

"Well, we're trained to recognize aircraft of all sorts – our own as well as those of the enemy. We maintain an alert for possible German spies, and especially U-Boat activity; it's called a watch and warn operation. But it's meant a lot of running around, making phone calls and the like."

"Good for you," says Willy. "Do you know if the U-Boat that was in Lunenburg is the same one that sank the minesweeper *Esquimault* outside of Halifax harbour a few months back?"

"Mid-April, that was," Frank interrupts, "just off Halifax harbour on a perfectly calm day – thirty-nine men lost. The ship went down so quick they weren't able to send out an SOS."

"No," says AB, "that was some other sub, but I don't know right offhand which one. Late in the war, few, if any of 'em, wore numbers on their conning towers. There's a dozen or more different types of U-Boats too, but like most things, there's usually particular markings that enable them to be identified. Plus, the Germans have always bragged about their kills, especially during the first half of the war when they were most successful."

"Well, we won't soon forget the loss of the *Caribou* ferry

in the fall of 1942 ... mid-October," recalls Frank. "She was torpedoed late at night and sunk on her regular run from Sydney to Port aux Basques – over a hundred men, women, and children lost. Many fishermen, Newfoundlanders fishin' out of Lunenburg and headin' home for Christmas, were among them. The ferry had a minesweeper escort, but there wasn't a whole lot they could do after the ferry was hit. Heartbreakin'."

"Night is the worst time of all to be travelling at sea. U-Boats can spend a lot of time on the surface chargin' their batteries without fear of being seen by air patrols," offers AB.

"And in that same year, one of them Lady Boats, *Lady Hawkins* I think it was, was torpedoed down off Cape Hatteras. More than two hundred people were lost that time, including June Knock. She was from Riverport – a nurse," says Frank.

"We've been tied to this awful business one way or another for a long time," says AB, doubtless thinking of his own daughters. "We play our parts, best we can. But thank God this war is over."

"One thing sure, the Norwegians will be happier now. Camp Norway is set to close in November. That'll be a loss to the town, for they have over fifty staff at their naval barracks. They've made a lot of friends throughout the area. You know, the Norwegian army, and their navy too, made use of the camp during the war."

"Some of 'em mightn't want to go back to Norway," says Roy. "Quite a number have married local women and started families. They practically took over Zion Lutheran Church in Lunenburg. They're more than welcome here. A lot of 'em will likely stay on after the camp closes. Many have jobs in shipbuilding, and my neighbour, Otto Zinck, he tells me there are several Norwegian engineers working in the Lunenburg Foundry."

"I heard the RCMP is goin' to take over the base for trainin' purposes after the Norwegians pull out," says Titus. "They want to try and make sure rum-runnin' doesn't start up again."

"Ha! It's not likely they'll ever cut it out altogether. But at least they won't have to go around chasin' up rumours of U-Boats," says AB.

"You know," says Roy, "we lost more than a few ships to U-Boats in the First World War too. 'Course there were a lot more schooners around then. We lost way more schooners in the Great War."

"Are you sure about that? I know the *Mona Marie* and the *Lucille M.* were both lost to U-Boats in '42."

"Yeah, we lost way more schooners in the first than in the war just ended. It's ancient history now, but we know how Captain Irwin Eisenhauer lost the *Elsie Porter* to a U-Boat. Then there was the *Potentate*, and I don't know how many others. The *Gladys M. Hollett* went down back in early August 1918."

"We should try and get our good neighbour Captain Bertie to tell us about the experience he had back in July 1918," says Frank. "They say he rescued about twenty men whose steamer was torpedoed down in the Caribbean. He was captain of *Moween* at the time, another of Boehner's new schooners working for the LaHave Outfitting Company. They was headed for Bermuda. I forget the name of the steamer, but the men were marooned in lifeboats for over two days when Bertie met up with them. We should get after him sometime to tell us about it."

"He never says very much, does he? Keeps things pretty much to hisself."

"Anyway, like I was sayin', the *Hollett* was just one of over half a dozen schooners sunk in 1918 by the Germans during the month of August alone," says Roy.

"Well, at least nobody on her was killed, and didn't they eventually refloat her?" says Titus.

To which Roy replies, "Yes, you're right, my mistake. The Germans first stripped her of everything before trying to sink her. She was later salvaged and put back in service."

"That was sort of standard procedure with the U-Boats, far from port as they were. No handy grocery store like this to stop by and yarn, hey, Arthur?" Willy laughs.

"They wouldn't ha' got much help from me," AB answers, "even if I'd been in business at the time, which I wasn't. As I said, the ADC only got going in 1940. Our job as volunteers during this last war has been mainly to report any sightings of submarines and strange aircraft in the vicinity of our observation post. We telephoned any sightings as soon as possible to Eastern Air Command. If fishermen reported any sign of a U-Boat, this would be relayed to HQ. But mostly our reports dealt mainly with information on any aircraft seen or heard."

"Did you have much success?" asks Frank.

"I can only hope so. Eastern Command gave us increased support this last couple of years, so they must have thought it worthwhile. The thing is, unlike World War I, during this last war we built up a large marine force – but it was pretty much dedicated to the defense of England and protection of the convoys. We've had very few vessels available to defend shipping along our own shore. So all this time, U-Boats have been sinking ships left and right, mostly freighters, one after the other."

"Easy pickin's … the idea being to cut off the food supply, supplies of everything, to England," is Willy's comment.

"In our shallow waters, submarines worked to the Germans' advantage. They could park on the bottom close to shore – like happened to the *Esquimault* – out of sight, hard to detect by our ships, while they wait a chance to attack."

"It was probably much the same in the first war," says Roy. "I know we came close enough to it on one crossing."

"What crossing?" asks Frank.

"It was on a trip acrost to France. We was delivering fish to the French back then," says Roy.

"How's that?"

"Well, see, all those Frenchies have to eat fish on Friday. The Pope says so, and they listen, otherwise they're libel for Hell and damnation. So that was what a good many of us did during the first war – playin' God … helped to save the French. Much the same practice was carried out during this last one too. Feedin' Europe, as they say, but you know, the prices we been gettin' up to now have never been better."

"That's true. But a captain needs a special license, what they call a deep water ticket, to sail over there," says Titus.

"I sailed with Rollie Knickle back in 1915, I believe it was, in November. Anyways, he must ha' had the right ticket, for we made the trip a couple a' times. I remember on one crossing we spotted a U-Boat on the surface, but it was headed west. It was blowin' half a gale from the nor'west at the time, and the *Vivien P. Smith* was just flyin' along, I'd guess ten to twelve knots. Goin' the other way of course … east'ards. Anyways, we had no trouble getting to France on that trip.

"We delivered our cargo of salt cod in Marseilles and picked up a cargo of salt for the return voyage. It was on our way out of port that a French submarine stopped us. Everyone was ordered on deck for inspection. See, they were lookin' for German spies.

"Well, sir, there we was, all rigged out in our best, not havin' been messin' around cleanin' and saltin' down cod for close on two months. Done up right smart we was. But our cook on that trip was Moyle Schwartz – we called him Chock – a regular giant of a man, and one of Lunenburg's best cooks."

"Wasn't he cook with Angus Walters on the maiden voyage of the *Bluenose* in 1921?" asks Frank.

"That's right, so he was. But the French submarine captain picked him out straight away. He said, 'This man's obviously a Bosche. He will have to come with us."

"Now, most of you know Captain Rollie Knickle. He's no man to fool with. He's smart and he's been lucky, and he'll always stand up for you. And he stood up for Chock right then and there. I can still hear him, respectful like, as he spoke to that Frenchman, 'I can tell you, sir,' he said, 'that if you take that man prisoner, you will have to take all my men. We won't sail without that cook.' And that was the end of it, we was allowed to sail."

"He gave in?"

"That's Captain Rollie Knickle for you. I made many a trip with him."

"But, you know, some fishermen in Lunenburg County are still under suspicion by our own government – never mind the French – of sidin' with the Germans. Some of those captains, like Eisenhauer and Gerhardt, can still speak the old Dutch," said Frank.

"Dutch or Deutsch, call it what you like, but both of those captains had a schooner scuttled by the Germans."

"Hey, it's getting on to ten o'clock," says AB, with a quick look at the clock. I'm closing up now. Here, Austin, don't forget the salt you wanted."

"Well, at least that's not been rationed," Austin comments, adding, "Rationin' should come to an end pretty soon now, shouldn't it?"

"Might take a while," says AB.

Tugboat Trauma (November 20, 1946)

"How are you, Titus?" says AB, from his stand near the counter. "How are things at home? Have a good trip?" Then, perceiving that Titus had a purchase in mind, adds, "Can I get you something?"

"I'd like a box of pilot biscuits and a big bottle of ginger ale."

"For your young fellow, I expect?"

"Yeah. I had no idea the news travelled so fast."

"How is he anyway?" asks Frank. "Dr. Barss was in here earlier to stock up on his favourite cheese. He said he patched up your boy yesterday ... put in ten stitches."

"Oh, he'll be okay, but it was a close thing, you know."

"Tell us about it," says Willy, for he too heard the news.

"Well, I shouldn't stay too long. Oh, and I'd like a pound of brown sugar too."

"No problem," says AB, as he sets about making up the order. "I saw your boys passing by here about one o'clock yesterday. George was carrying his brother, saddled sort of piggyback. He went by at a run. The little guy had a cloth wound 'round the top of his head, and was hanging on like a starfish. I don't believe they even saw me. I was workin' outside gettin' some coal in at the time."

"Seems they were scufflin' while doin' up the dishes in the kitchen," says Titus. "The usual thing ... brothers, you know ... well, I guess Willy here doesn't know, but I'd imagine Frank knows how it goes."

"Yeah, I do," says Frank. "They're at it all the time. Thursa an' me got three of 'em."

"My wife tells me our kids are little angels when I'm home, but when I'm away at sea she's says it's a completely different story," says William.

"David, he doesn't like takin' orders from anybody," says Titus. "And George, I guess he took hold of him and dragged him back to dry the dishes. It was our big butcher knife that got David behind his right ear, George being left-handed and all – made a pretty good cut. Missed the jugular by this much," says Titus, straining to allow a slight space for light to pass between his thumb and forefinger. "Took a piece out of the right ear as well."

"That could just as well been the end of him," says Austin.

"Austin says he saw the two of 'em goin' up the road. Neither of us knew what was up."

"I only found out about it this mornin' when I got home," says Titus. "The wife had quite a scare yesterday, though, after it happened. She was at a meetin' up at the church and someone rushed in to tell her that one of her boys had been cut. She thought they said 'killed,' and that pretty well did her in on the spot. Anyways, the ether has worn off, and the young fella's comin' around. George feels pretty bad about it, as you can imagine. I'd better be gettin' home with this stuff."

"Don't take much for women to faint," says William, as Titus makes his way out the door. "I know my mother, Frances, fainted dead away when the minister came by to tell her my brother Donnie was lost at sea. She was hangin' out wash at the time, out back of the house. She dropped down in front of him, right under the wash line."

"Small wonder," says AB under his breath.

"Now there's where a telephone would ha' come in handy

... might have made a difference for the poor woman," says Roy. "That way the minister could have phoned to warn her he was plannin' to come for a visit."

"It wouldn't ha' made much difference for poor Donnie," says Willy.

"Now you might not believe this," says William, "but the very same thing happened four or five years later when my other brother Ralph was lost at sea. 'Frances,' says the minister, 'I've got some terrible news.' And my poor old mother, she drops down on the spot under the wash line. Like Donnie, Ralph's body was never recovered."

"That wash line must be hexed," offers Roy by way of explanation.

"Could be. Why, only last year when I was away on a trip, didn't the minister come down the hill on his bicycle on a friendly visit to see my mother. As soon as she saw him comin' – and yes, she was hangin' out wash – she fainted on the spot. Anyway, they drug her in the house and brought her around. She recovered all right from that. But I don't think the minister will ever even consider comin' by here again."

"A doctor's not much use at times like that," says Roy, after a pause given over to a lot of communal head shaking.

"Not much anyone can do about it."

"But we're lucky, you know, to have a man like Dr. Barss on hand for emergencies," says AB. "I know he's helped Carrie and me off the hook more 'n once."

"I always said that man's one smart old doctor," says Frank, as a familiar figure enters The Shop and enthusiastically hails the gathering.

"Hey there, Uncle Arthur. Good to see you again! And good evening to all of you fine fellows!"

"It's Kenny! Kenny Lohnes, you made it home! We'd near given you up for lost," exclaims AB, stepping forward smartly to hug his favourite nephew.

"Heard you were open this evening so thought to drop in ... surprise you, like."

"Welcome home!" sounds the hearty chorus from the gathering in AB's on this snowy Wednesday evening.

"Well, I'm glad to be here, and that's for sure and certain," answers the young seaman, patting his middle. "Lost a bit of weight over the last week or so."

"More like two weeks, wasn't it? Paper said you parted company with your tow, when was it? – November fifth, and you just got ashore a day or so ago."

"They towed me in to Shelburne on Saturday, the sixteenth."

"How much did you drop anyways?"

"I'm down to two hundred now, so all told, I lost about sixty pounds."

"Who cares how much weight he lost? That trip could ha' been the end of him," says Frank, who had seen more than his share of hard times at sea.

As Kenny plops himself on the chair proffered by Frank, AB hastens to bring out another from behind the counter. Pipes, including Kenny's own, are stoked afresh as the group settles themselves comfortably in anticipation of a good yarn. One of their own, Kenny was a friendly familiar figure in the district, and one not backward in coming forward.

Gradually the shuffling eases, as the old blue enamelled pot-bellied stove radiates a comfortable glow from a cluster of winking red coals behind the clear mica windows.

"So, did you miss me?" Kenny jokes, attempting to make light of his recent harrowing experience. "I heard a commemoration service in my honour was planned at the church this Sunday, did I hear right? Looks like I'm on time for that."

"Well," AB hedges, "we were thinking about it pretty seriously. Truth is, we had it pretty well all arranged. You gave us a good scare, Kenny. It's been twenty-five years since your uncle Calvin was lost overboard on the *Ruby L. Pentz*. We didn't want to have to go through that kind of experience again. Thank God you made it back."

"I'd have been better off to have stayed home this fall. It

was the first time I shipped out since last spring. See, I caught pneumonia and was laid up all summer. Then they asked me to babysit this tug, *Tanac 261*, one of about a dozen built in Lunenburg. So I figured, nothing to it, I can do this. It was supposed to be a short and simple trip from Lunenburg down to Liverpool."

"A one-man crew?" someone asks.

"Yeah, a one-man crew. And it was the same on the other two tugs. All three of us were being towed by a much larger tug, the *Glenfield*, down to Liverpool for repairs and a shining up. They'll likely all be sold before long.

"It was some slow going, I can tell you. But then one thing after another happened. That's always the way of it, ain't it, though? First thing it come on to blow, a regular howling gale. And snow! Next thing the tow rope, a nine-and-a-half-inch hawser, you, broke."

"It must have been an old one."

"Rotten, it had to be rotten to part that easy. And the same thing happened to the other two tugs. The first day I drifted along so close to land, I could make out the shoreline. And I saw the *Glenfield* pick up the other two tugs singly. I couldn't understand why they didn't come back for me. But I never lost hope and always kept faith that they would come back."

"But they never did?"

"No, they didn't. They say it took 'em about two and a half hours to recover the other two tugs, and by that time *Tanac 261* was lost to their sight. Mountainous seas built up, and they stayed up. The real trouble was, the alarm was raised only late on the fifth of the month. So there I was, dancin' along like a cork, for days and nights on end."

"Ten, by all accounts," says AB.

"That's about right. The worst time of all was when the boat took in water. See, I had nothin' to use as a sea anchor, to keep her head to the wind except the regular two anchors. That lasted only a couple of hours before both ropes parted. After that, it was pitch and roll, pitch and roll. I figured for sure I'd die. On the worst windy days, it was only by constant bailing I managed to keep her from swamping."

"Couldn't the engine be started?" someone asks.

"Well, the problem is, I'm not a diesel engineer. But when you're dumb, you just try and get 'em started. For two whole days I kept at it, and finally got it going. I steered by the sun, on a northwest heading, but after about four hours ran out of fuel. After that, there wasn't anything I could do at the wheel. At night, I managed to get a few hours of rest, off and on. It was rough, but I never altogether lost hope."

"Did you try signalling other ships to come by and help you?"

"I conserved fuel as best I could, for the auxiliary motors and generators, so I could show signal lights at night. In the daytime, I rigged sheets at the masthead in hopes of rescue."

"Did you know that RCAF planes were out searching for you?" AB asks.

"Well, I might have heard an airplane once, but I couldn't be sure. But ships, I saw a few steam by. One was only five or six miles distant. No sooner did they heave in sight than they disappeared from view – heartbreaking. I've been told the *Glenfield* returned from Liverpool to join in the hunt, as well as a good many other surface craft. And I'm grateful to everyone for that. But there's a lot of ocean out there. When I saw that Yankee Coast Guard cutter, *Pontchartrain*, bearing down on me on the last day I said to myself, 'Kenny, you're a lucky man. You're goin' home soon and have a hot meal.'"

"You're lucky compared to that small two-master, the *Frances Robie*, from the Bay of Islands. She disappeared on her way home from Halifax a day or so before you left Lunenburg for Liverpool. There's been no sign of her or her four-man crew. She's a fifty-foot Newfoundland motor schooner."

"She's even smaller than the *Tanac 261*," says Kenny. "*Tanac*'s all of sixty-five feet."

'You say you lost sixty pounds, Kenny. What did you survive on all that time?"

"Not a whole lot, but I rationed out what little I had – a half-dozen apples and a box of cookies. For drinking water I drained a couple of buckets of rusty water from the engine. If it hadn't been for that I might not be alive today. I was some happy when I saw the *Pontchartrain*. They told me they used radar to locate me, and that was sixty-five miles south of Yarmouth. *Tanac* drifted about a hundred and fifty miles altogether. The coast guard took me in tow, and twenty miles from Shelburne a tug took over."

AB recalled his own difficult early problems at sea – altogether different than those of his nephew, though he probably felt at least as close to death then as Kenny ever did on the tug. "And here we went to all the trouble, the day before yesterday, planning out a special service to commemorate your passing. We were all set to ring the church bell. How many is it now? Would twenty-three bongs be about right?"

"Yes, twenty-three bongs and two or three bings should just about do it. But please hold off a while. It's awful nice of you to think of me, but if it's just the same with you I'd like to think my death has been postponed indefinitely."

"We hope, for a very long time."

"What I don't understand is how come so many tugs have been built in Lunenburg. They're no good for fishin'," Austin speaks up.

"Well, I can answer that," offers Kenny. "It was a wartime project contracted to Smith and Rhuland by the British Ministry of War Transport. It's hard to believe, I know, but I'm told over two hundred and fifty tugs were built in Canadian shipyards. The one that took me for a ride is number 261. She was built in Lunenburg along with ten or eleven others, exactly the same. The first two were built for the RCAF as marine rescue craft. The ones made in Lunenburg are all of wood. Most of the others, I understand, are steel-hulled. *Tanac 261* is practically brand new – built early last year."

"So, Kenny, when will you be ready for sea again?" asks Frank.

"Well, mister man, I'll tell you now. Sometime, maybe in the middle of summer, when the sea is smooth and there are plenty of hams aboard with me. But I'll never travel alone at sea again."

Guest Speaker (1947)

Roy and Titus got an early start loafing on this evening in late October, 1947. While talking, they slowly move on up the road towards The Shop.

Roy says, "Do you remember last year when my wife got sick and I stayed home for a month or so 'til she recovered?"

"Yes I do. You missed out on that good trip we had with Joey Wentzell."

"Pauline used to drop in, regular like, to help Letoile around the house. That girl changed a lot since she stayed with Florence and Perry. Last time she visited us I was busy doin' barn work … it was during haymakin'. One of your young fellers helped out with the hayin'. Well, after that, Pauline went off to Halifax to start work, some sort of office work I think it was. No, it was a job in Simpson's she got."

"That's good. It's not all that easy now, for a girl startin' out."

"Well, I agree, but the trouble was, she met a scheister off a navy ship, name of Ray, at least that's what he called himself the one time he came down to Lower Rose Bay. Anyways, he talked her into marrying him, least that's what I heard. He's a real mouth artist – talked a blue streak. But he's shrewd, and slimy, and didn't tell anyone very much about himself and his family. Nobody, including Pauline, seems to know much about him."

"Well, that don't sound right."

"I'll say. The trouble is, Pauline has returned to Lower Rose Bay, pregnant. Bernard and Mabel are good-hearted people. They're a kindly couple, and have taken her in for the long haul."

"So her husband, this so-called Ray, where's he at?"

"Good question. They say he took off for Toronto. Pauline even went up there and spent the better part of a soul-destroyin' week trying to find him … followin' up hopeless leads. Can you imagine what a heartbreakin' experience that would be for a young girl like that? Then she got home only to find out that he's already a married man."

"Oh my! Now she's left on her own, with little or nothing."

"I'm afraid so. …and a baby on the way. You got to feel sorry for her, but what can one do?"

"Not a whole lot one can do about it. She'll have to see it out. It happens all too often. At least she's with a good family. Look, you, you don't have to go to a big city to find scheisters like this Ray character."

"You're right there. My brother Bernie's youngest girl, Dorothy, went and got herself pregnant early this year."

"Now Roy, you know that's pretty hard to do," says Titus, interrupting his neighbour.

"You know what I mean, Titus. They say she got over-friendly with some local men working along the road. And there's more than one of us in Rose Bay knows who's responsible."

"I have a fairly good idea. I know the car. Early last spring I had to lay a plank across the front of my driveway to keep him from wearin' it out, usin' it to turn around in, time after time after time. Back and forth he'd go, back and forth, half the night long, so's he could pass in front of Bernie's place – lookin' for her to come out to be picked up, I suppose. It got to be pretty damn annoying. And him a married man, with children of his own. It's Duffer we're takin' about here, right? Lives up above the Crossroads?"

Roy nods in reluctant acknowledgement.

"And that's not the worst of it. Late on, Dorothy went and got a maid's job in Kingsburg, and didn't she go and die in childbirth. Fifteen years old she was!"

"There ought to be a law," says Titus. "The best thing we can do is to try and bring our girls up right in the first place."

"I can think of something Rudy Duffer could do," says Roy. "He could go jump into a well and drown himself like that fellow Lewis Randall done years ago over in Upper LaHave. When his wife found out he'd made a schoolgirl pregnant, he went and committed suicide. I remember the death notice read something like 'Presumed to have fallen into his well while drawing water.' Not bloody likely. I might even believe it, except that Mrs. Helen Crouse makes no secret of the fact there was no bucket in the well! Well, at least Lewis had a conscience, and some members of his family apparently didn't object to lettin' the world know the truth of the matter. I was shippin' out from West LaHave at the time and it was common knowledge over there."

"Messy business just the same, all 'round," says Titus. "Wouldn't ever do to drink the water from that well again."

As the two men entered The Shop it was clear they were among the last of the loafers to arrive. Evidently, the program, such as it was, had already begun. A distant relative and friend of AB's family had arrived to pay his respects.

Captain Aubrey Backman had many relatives in Riverport and District. He was a cousin to AB's mother Elmina. Several among the company knew him as a former shipmate. But he was recognized as an old hand in more ways than one, not least of which was age, years at sea, years in the services, and, though he got a late start, years as a rum-runner. No matter how you'd look at it, the man was a survivor.

In brief, he'd done it all. He served several years with the merchant marine, then sailed salt bank schooners fishing fish before making the switch to bottle fishing, against the wishes of his wife and mother. The reason given, which he would repeat this evening as on numerous other occasions, was because "the money was too good, and he had a family to support." Then, throughout World War II, he served as a lieutenant on convoy duty with the Royal Canadian Navy. Although he could tell a good yarn, Aubrey seldom had much to say about wars, except for the rum war during Prohibition, as this evening's get-together would bear out. In fact, he seemed quite agreeable to do so, in response to Carmen's invitation, shortly after entering The Shop.

"Look, when I joined in 1929, it was already late in the business. But a mate's wages for one month of fishing was eighty-five dollars. As a captain, runnin' rum, a man could make five hundred a month, with bonuses on top of that."

Titus and his neighbour Roy Deal hold their peace. They have their reasons. Titus never made good in rum-running. And, although Roy had always expressed his interest, he had no experience in smuggling. Roy never went rum-running. His wife, Letoile, objected too strongly. But this evening every man's interest in the visitor's yarns is transparent.

Aubrey continues, "I got off to a slow start. There were a couple of trips on the *Ocean Maid*. Then I was assigned to pick up the *Symore*, a fish dragger, to take her to Liverpool to have her converted for rum-running. The new engine in her was good for twelve knots. We managed to make two drops along the Jersey coast from St. Pierre before we got into trouble. The Yanks thought they owned the North Atlantic that summer. They sank three rum boats, all of them in international waters, forty to sixty miles off the American coast."

"And yours was one of 'em?" Frank asks.

"Yes," answers Aubrey, "that was off Nantucket Light. We played cat and mouse for a while, but in the end they rammed us about ten feet ahead of the wheelhouse. Lost two dories and the port hatch cover. The American cutter, the *Legale* or *Legare* I think she was, then backed out of the collision and laid about fifty yards off our port side. I checked the *Symore*, and found she couldn't be saved. I then called the cutter alongside and transferred our crew to the cutter. *Symore* and four thousand cases of liquor sank in about nine minutes, one mile off Nantucket Light and forty miles off the coast. The cutter then proceeded to take us to Connecticut, the New London Coast Guard station."

"What happened after that?" Carmen asks.

"Well, there were some pretty harsh words between us which were never reported. Of course, nothing ever came of it, though that time we lost our ship and the cargo as well.

"But you know, not all the cutter captains were hard-asses. Some would get involved and earn much more money rum-running than they were being paid to police the coast. Some cutters would throw a chunk of coal on board of a rum boat ordering so many cases, seven hundred in one example that I know of. The cutter then came out and would load on their liquor when the rum boat had their order aside. The cutter would in turn, along with the money, bring back clothes from the mainland wished for by the rum-running crew.

"After that mess with the *Symore* was cleaned up, I proceeded to Buzzard Bay to check out an important drop we planned to use during the winter months. That drop had been worked for all of eight years. But it didn't work out for us. The Coast Guard found it and was keeping a very close eye on the place. I reported this to the station, and everything was closed down. The radio set was taken out of the building, and all hands took off for the woods."

"Who was in charge of the whole operation anyway?" asks Roy, though no one present really expected an answer.

"Can't really say for sure, but one of the big names was a guy in Jersey named Borden. He had a lot to do with the trade. Anyways, I managed to get home, and was assigned to the *Reo II*."

"That was one of Spinny's old boats, wasn't it?" asks Frank.

"Yes, that's right. I know of Spinny, but I never met him. I was sort of hoping I might meet him here tonight."

"Spinny does his loafing down in Rissers' store or at Ritcey and Creasers – he hardly ever comes here," Carmen says.

"*Reo II* had a lot of captains – seven that I know of. The very first one was Freeman Beck. When I had her, she was hired by two guys from New Jersey. We loaded up at St. Pierre and proceeded to a position about fifteen miles off a New Jersey beach, just a short distance south of New York harbour. We were picked up several times at that position and it became known to the cutters.

"I asked the two guys several times to change the position. They would not listen. The next time we came into position, the cutters had a trap set for us. They formed a triangle, with us in the centre. When we arrived a speedboat came inside for four hundred cases. We had twelve cases in the boat when the cutter's search light came on. I started *Reo*'s engine and covered the speedboat from the cutter's light while they dumped the twelve cases. Shortly after, the speedboat got tangled up with another cutter and was taken in tow for runnin' without lights. She had to pay a fine of four hundred dollars.

"Anyway, getting back to my story, one cutter's searchlight and gun were trained on us until the speedboat was searched and no liquor found. We gave the cutter the slip off Nantucket Light, and *Reo II* was unloaded and returned to Yarmouth."

"Where did that name *Reo* come from anyway?" Roy asks Aubrey.

"Not sure."

"I can answer that," says Carmen. "We were talking about that in the garage just a week or so ago. Lester and Donnie said it was an early American car. I remember them saying it had a special badge and a temperature gauge, both with wings on the grill."

"Wings? Imagine that," replies Aubrey with a slight touch of sarcasm. "Well, *Reo I*, the original boat, might have had wings compared to *Reo II*. But her wings were clipped when one of her two engines was removed and installed in *Reo II*. *Reo II* was built in 1931, especially for rum-running. Her top speed was ten knots, but I got to say, she was a workhorse.

"Another time we were lying over there on the coast off Buzzard Bay in fine weather. We had *Reo II* all painted up while the coast guard cutter watched us. When we were finished, the Coast Guard had four bottles of mixed black paint, and they broke these over the ship's house. I decided I could throw rocks just as well as they could throw paint bottles. So the next time we went out to St. Pierre I got myself two baskets of nice small beach rocks and put one basket forward and one aft.

"Two trips later we were lying off the coast with an American cutter when she decided to give us a washing down with one of her hoses. When she got about twenty feet from us, I could see the captain looking out the wheelhouse window with a big grin on his face. I took aim for him with a nice round beach rock. I missed him, but it went through the next window beside him. He got out of there in a hurry. Those beach rocks stayed in the *Reo* 'til we laid up in Yarmouth for good.

"During the winters of 1932 and 1933 we were chased off the American coast by cutters several times. Sometimes it got pretty hot. They would make sweeps over the *Reo* with a machine gun. There was one bullet hole in the mainmast fourteen inches above the wheelhouse. That's gettin' a bit too close. I was some happy when we swung for Yarmouth the last time. I quit 'round about the time Prohibition ended. Some fellas, like Carmen here, kept on long afterwards and managed not to get caught."

"Yeah, I been lucky, cornered sometimes but never trapped. Not like Titus, you, he run into big trouble. When was that, Titus ... 1936, wasn't it?"

"Titus? No, that can't be. You were never into rum-runnin', were you?" exclaims Austin, thoroughly aroused by this revelation. Titus says nothing, but Aubrey sits by, ready with some details.

"I remember now, yes, you were with Captain George

Lohnes on the *Miserinko* when a cutter nabbed you on the coast down off New Hampshire. It was the *Harriet Jane*, the same Coast Guard cutter that gave us a washing down over in Buzzard Bay back in '32. *Miserinko*, she was built in 1931, the same year as *Reo II*, both in Meteghan. Who was mate with Lohnes at that time, Titus?"

"Herbert Knickle was mate, an' Westhaver, Harold Westhaver, was engineer," says Titus, realizing there was no way out of owning up to what he knew to these old hands.

"Lohnes and Knickle both got nearly a year of jail time," says Aubrey. "Trouble was, an American fella in New Jersey, Ralph Bitters, owned the *Miserinko*. That complicated the case for their early release as requested by the British Ambassador to the U.S. Secretary of State. The boat was known to the U.S. Coast Guard as a "Bitters Boat." The Americans saw the owner as clearly violating the Tariff Act, no matter what the British Admiralty had to say about it."

"How about you, Titus, did you do time as well?" Carmen asks. Everyone is looking at Titus expectantly, though in Austin's case disbelief overlays anticipation. Secrets will out in a loafers' lair. AB could scarcely credit all he'd been hearing this evening. Quietly stunned, he said little, but glanced toward the clock secretly wishing he had an excuse to cut off proceedings. But no, it would never do to interrupt or hurry it along.

As for Titus, well, his wife knew about the time he had spent in the pen. How could she not? She had been left on her own with two young children for over three months – May through July, 1936 – while he was locked up down in the States. She knew all about that unfortunate episode – "never again," she had made him vow. In later years, I recall her joking in a weak moment about our father having done time once upon a time in Sing Sing prison during rum-running.

"Me and a crew member, Bronson Cluett, were released just short of our three-month term. We came home together," Titus replies. "Don't know about the rest of the crew."

"*Reo II* was involved in that incident," says Aubrey. "She was the warehouse boat that supplied *Miserinko* with alcohol before the Coast Guard cornered her. *Reo II* could handle an enormous load – up to eight thousand cases." Titus simply nods in agreement, taking small private pleasure knowing his brother-in-law, Spinny – Winfred "Teddy" Spindler – had not been the captain of the *Reo II* at that particular point in time. He would have been way better off on *Reo II* than on *Miserinko*, he thinks. Unfortunately, that never happened. Spinny, for whatever reason, didn't like him enough to take him along with him as cook on the *Reo*.

"I can't think who might have been captain of the *Reo* in early 1936," says Aubrey. "I got out of the business when Prohibition ended. Do you happen to know, Carmen?"

"No, I don't."

"A lot of liquor in that boat. Like I said, she was a workhorse."

"The *Ocean Maid*, one of my earliest boats, delivered nine thousand four hundred cases, *Symore* four thousand two hundred, and *Reo II* thirty-eight thousand cases of liquor under my command. That's what, let me see," says Aubrey. "Let's say over fifty thousand cases carried to drop points on the American coast. So, for sinking *Symore* forty-two miles offshore while we were in international waters, I feel like that's been partly paid for."

"In total, fifty-one thousand six hundred cases," says AB, playing accountant, shaking his head in disbelief that God-fearing men in his community should have engaged in such illegal commerce, and on such a scale. It's not my place to speak out, he thinks ... wouldn't do any good if I did.

"*Reo II* is still paying her way, I hear," says Frank, interrupting AB's train of thought, as everyone eases back from the edge of their chairs.

"How's that? During the war, wasn't she taken over by the navy and rigged out as a minesweeper?" Titus asks. Old soldier that he was, he always did his best to keep up with the news. "What became of her at war's end?"

"Last thing I heard, she'd been declared surplus and sold by the government to Newfoundland for thirteen thousand dollars," says Frank.

"That's true," says Aubrey, "and that's where she is now – in service as a coastal freighter operating out of Grand Bank, Newfoundland. Could be she's still doin' business on the sly, though. You never know."

"Maybe," says Frank, "but that's getting pretty hard to do now that the marine section of the RCMP have taken over Camp Norway. I hear they're using it as a training base, and have minesweepers to patrol the coastal waters."

"I know some of them Norwegians are hangin' on here planning to continue their whale hunting. Fella named Karl Karlson has started up a factory over in Blandford for extracting the oil from whales caught offshore. From what I've heard, they're makin' a go of it. No reason why they shouldn't. We've never bothered going after whales, but I see 'em all the time steamin' along either side of Cross Island goin' to who knows where. There's no shortage of whales in our waters," says Willy.

"They can have the whales. I reckon I might stick to fishin' fish for now. Good to see all of you again," says Aubrey with a chuckle, as he notices AB moving to close up. As a body, he and his fellow loafers rise to retrieve coats and hats.

Lightning Strikes (1948)

"They're still shovellin' out the roads to Upper and Lower Kingsburg. An' it's been two weeks since the storm set in."

"Who says that?" Titus asks his shipmate, Roy Deal.

"Letoile didn't say who. It's just news makin' the rounds on the phone. The family takes turns listen' in. It's the only entertainment we have. Progress on the shovellin' job gets reported on yard by yard. You an' Helen ought to give in an' get a phone, Titus." Roy takes his time lighting his pipe as he watches to see how Titus reacts to this oft-mentioned suggestion. But, as usual, it falls on deaf ears.

"Humpf! We worked in relays to shovel out the road right down to Lower Rose Bay. We was at it three days in a row. If they'd get around to pavin' the thing it would make life a lot easier. Not that it's gonna happen in a hurry even though the province has a new PC leader in Bob Stanfield."

"At least they got the road done from Lunenburg to Riverport this year. But we pay taxes too. There must be more Liberals in Riverport than there is down our way," says Willy. "We're long overdue a change in government in this province."

Titus happens to have more on his mind than politics, and for once he ignores the invitation to continue Willy's argument. "But it's true, we could ha' used a phone at our place just before Christmas. My brother Albert got his leg broke on the road out in front of our place. A young fool from Kingsburg, what's his name, some Knock, got his car stuck tryin' to make it through the drifts. So of course, we all turn out to try and help move him along. But nothin' doin'. Albert was pushin' behind the right back wheel when a plank of wood placed there for traction flew out and got him below the knee."

"I heard about that. How's he makin' out?"

"We carried him best we could into the house and laid him out on the kitchen couch. Knowin' no better, my youngest boy asked his Uncle Allie if he would like him to read a story while he rested. Albert showed little interest, as you can imagine, bein' in some pain. We made him comfortable as we could, and Dr. Barss – Allison, the young one – was summoned and made his way on foot to attend. Otto Zinck hitched up his ox team and we loaded Albert onto an ox cart and took him to the Crossroads. From there, a car took him to the Dawson Memorial in Bridgewater."

"Otto told me it was all he could do to get his team through the snow drifts," says Roy.

"We're awful lucky to have two doctors in the community," says AB. "Why, just last February during a snowstorm, Estelle, our eldest, had an acute appendicitis attack. The old Dr. Barss, Geoffrey, showed up and took control. He sent word to Amy Mossman, Titus's cousin, to come and help out. She's an RN. And she came, right away. The doctor didn't trust to move the child during such stormy conditions. He operated in the house, took her appendix out right there on our dining room table. And a year or two before that, he yanked out Margaret Jean's tonsils in the same spot."

"The radio says this storm is the worst in almost fifty years."

"That might have been the winter of the big snow in 1905, according to *The Chronicle Herald*," says AB, as he carefully adds coal to the lowering fire.

"Well, at least the mail service is back again. We're open

for business. And you must all have heard the new radio station, CKBW, is up and runnin'," says Austin.

"Anybody know if either of the stations ever reported on the lightning strike at our school?"

"CKBW made their first broadcast on Christmas Eve, didn't they?"

"Yes, they did," says AB, who seems to always be up on the news. "They were too late to report on the lightning strike, but CHNS might have. I'm not sure. It should have made the headlines, though I don't recall seeing much if anything about it in the local papers. People were probably too busy getting ready for Christmas. That business gets earlier every year."

"Talkin' about headlines, did you hear what happened to Murdock Getson over in LaHave?" asks Roy.

"Captain Getson? I saw his obit in the paper. He was a well-respected old sea captain. He could ha' died of old age," says Frank.

"Well, he wasn't that old – only sixty-two. But it's how he died that's interesting," says Roy, knocking out his pipe in the coal scuttle, after checking carefully there's no coal left in it.

"Oh, an' how did he go?" Austin asks.

"The strange thing is the doctor had given him a clean bill of health early on the very day he passed away. See this?" says Roy as he points to his pipe while he tamps down a fresh charge of tobacco. "He was out loafing at Publicover's store over in LaHave. They say he stopped while tellin' a story, to refill his pipe when, all of a sudden, he just keeled over dead, right in his chair."

"You take it easy there, Roy," Willy advises. "But I suppose that's as good a way to go as any I can think of."

"I can think of worse," says Titus.

"Getting struck by lightning would end things pretty quick, I'd imagine."

"Kind of tough all the same for family members, so close to Christmas and all," says AB, ever a moderating influence on the gathering.

"They'll want to go a little easy on the jingle bells," Austin suggests.

"My young feller got me up to watch the lightnin' with him that night when the school got struck," says Titus. "We watched for a while together from his sister Carolyn's bedroom. That's on the north side of our house, see. She was away in New Brunswick at Mount Allison University at the time. We could tell the storm was gettin' closer ... shorter and shorter time between the flash and the boom. Then, as we watched, we saw this orange-yellow ball of fire driftin' slowly down from the sky, right lazy-like, taking it's time fallin' to earth. Then crack! A moment after it disappeared, there was a tremendous blast. I figured it might have knocked off a church steeple."

"No, our church steeple's been spared," says Austin, "but the Presbyterian steeple was knocked off by lightning two different times, I think. Funny thing that ... the Lutheran church bein' right across the road from the Presbyterian, and on higher ground too. The two churches used to be in the same building where the Lutheran church now stands, weren't they?"

AB, as a preeminent elder in the Lutheran church, knows the facts of these sorts of matters. "That's true, Austin," he says. "The two congregations joined forces in 1843 to build a Union Church. But the Presbyterians wanted their own church and by 1890, they had built and dedicated Saint Andrew's across the road from the Lutheran church.

"They must ha' wanted it pretty bad," says Austin.

"The Presbyterians spared no effort to have their own building. There was a huge slab of granite – they called it 'the church rock' – on the hill above Moshers Settlement out in Upper Kingsburg, and that's what they quarried for stone – cracked it up and shaped the pieces for the foundation stones. The story goes their own minister, Rev. George Leck, worked along with his parishioners breaking and shaping the rock. They brought the foundation stones by ox wagon all the way from Upper Kingsburg. Titus, your people must ha' been involved with that work."

"Yes, I heard tell of it," says Titus.

"Well, there don't seem to be many other people who have."

"Lennox Conrad lives across the road from Trinity United Church, and he says that church is located in Riverport and not in Upper Rose Bay at all," says Austin.

"Is that so?" AB responds. "I won't waste anyone's time arguing about that. He's the Justice of the Peace. And it really doesn't matter to me where it is, as long as it is. We poor souls need all the help we can get."

"Sounds like there was a competition goin' on. But the Presbyterian steeple is the only one ever knocked off by lightning ... oncest or was it twice?" questions Austin.

Yes, it might have been. Last time was back in 1933, I believe."

"Has the Lutheran steeple ever been struck by lightning?"

"Not to my knowledge," says AB, tiring of Austin's questions.

"I'd sure like to know what the difference is between the Lutheran and Presbyterian and Methodist churches, aside from the spelling of the names," Austin continues relentlessly. "Does anybody know?" Silence reigns supreme for a few moments as he looks around.

"You should have been here earlier, Austin. Reverend Mawhinney, the Presbyterian minister, dropped by to stock up on some items. He's been coming by from time to time. I'm surprised you haven't run into him yet. He should be able to answer your questions," says AB.

"Wonder if he ever heard of the church rock," Frank says.

"He's an Irishman, ain't he?" says Roy.

"Yes, he says he grew up on a farm in a small village outside of Belfast in Northern Ireland. His first name is David but I don't know his middle name. Maybe he doesn't have one. He's a tall, straitlaced sort of fellow. Yesterday he walked down to The Shop through all this snow, rigged out in a suit and a tie, waistcoat, and, if you can believe it, a top hat."

"Wants to create a good impression, I guess."

"Nothing wrong with that – just a bit unusual. He wanted to know if I thought it's going to continue cold like this all winter. That manse is a big house and hard to heat. Don't know what the guy who built it was thinking. It's four stories high, and as for insulation, well, I doubt there's very much apart from a bit of seagrass an' old newspaper stuffed between the walls."

"Little or none at all, I'd imagine" says Willy.

"It wouldn't surprise me," AB continues. "Anyway, it's all new to their young fella too. He goes by the name of Lawrence, but I think his first name is David, same as his father. Lawrence is about the same age as your youngest, Titus. He'll be going to school with your boy. Back in the old country Reverend Mawhinney said they had a tiny house with only two bedrooms. Now they got more 'n they know what to do with. It's a huge old house, and when the wind gets up, like it's been in recent days, the place shakes and creaks like crazy, so he says. Young Lawrence is afraid of the dark and won't sleep unless they keep a light on in his room. He doesn't like going upstairs and is terrified of going into the attic.

"Reverend Mawhinney is one of several new clergymen from Ireland who volunteered their services in Canada – claims he was told there's a shortage here. Whether he plans to stay any length of time – that I can't tell you. Could be they'll have a job getting used to things around here."

"Oh, why would that be? Can't be all that different around here from Ireland, can it?" asks Austin.

"Well, I'll give you an example. Around New Years' they got a shock. Belsnicklers! They were scared out of their wits on the first evening when a bunch of Belsnicklers making the rounds dropped in on 'em. Apparently there's no such thing back in Ireland. Their outlandish-looking visitors were eventually able to reassure the Mawhinneys they meant no harm, though I doubt they were offered very much by way of the usual refreshment."

"I imagine that would be a bit of a shock to them – the Mawhinneys, I mean," says Austin.

"Did the Reverend ever tell you what he did before coming to Canada?" asks Frank.

"Yes, he used to be a grocer," AB answers, half-afraid of Austin's next question.

"A grocer!" exclaims Austin. "Just like you, AB. Why, he must have been converted. There's still time for you, AB, you're already an elder in the church. You could be a minister. Have you given any thought to it?"

"Don't talk such foolishness, Austin. For starters, Reverend Mawhinney's an educated man. I never got beyond grade seven."

"Why don't you join the ministry yourself, Austin? You're good at preachin'. Or haven't you seen the light yet?" says Willy, taking the pressure off AB, much to the latter's relief.

"Oh, don't you worry about me. I've seen the light. The Christmas story helps bring it into focus for true believers. And, Willy, if you don't believe it, then you'll never see the light. It's as simple as that," says Austin, slapping his knees for emphasis.

Even Titus senses things getting slightly out of hand, so he attempts to change the subject. "It's just as well no one tells Mawhinney about the steeple of his church being knocked off by lightning."

"His kid, Lawrence, will likely learn all about that when he sees what happened to the schoolhouse," Willy adds.

"Lightning Alley, that's what I'd call that area," says Frank. "The Lutherans must be livin' right."

"God's got nothing to do with it, if that's what you mean," says AB, scarcely masking his indignation at this touch of what in his eyes borders on blasphemy.

"Well," Frank adds, realizing that he'd better make amends quickly, "good thing The Shop is on low ground here. We can feel safe enough hangin' out here on a stormy Saturday evening. But a man could walk through the hole that lightning made in the south side of the school. Maybe it came down the chimney to the cast iron stove and went out the side of the building. Good thing school wasn't in when it happened."

"We're hoping to get that hole properly patched up in the next day or two," says Austin. "Despite the damage to the outside wall, the lower room doesn't show much damage. Virginia says the upstairs room where Miss Pentz teaches the higher grades wasn't damaged at all."

"All a matter of luck," says AB, clarifying his position on the phenomenon.

"Lightning Alley would be a very good name for this area," Frank repeats. "It's seen enough strikes to get me thinkin' about havin' a lightning rod attached to my house. Old Bertie's housekeeper, Frances Gaudley, across the road here tells about a glowing ball of lightning about six inches in diameter comin' right into her living room during a storm a year or so ago. Says she was just settin' there in her rocking chair when it came to rest on her hand. After a second or so it moved away and out of the room – scared her half to death."

"No damage done," says Austin, adding, "Could ha' maybe been a ghost. Maybe it was the ghost of her husband, Kenneth. Old Bertie now, he won't even consider puttin' a lightning rod up on the place. But then he's probably immune to lightning."

Displaced Persons and Refugees (1950)

"Hey, you know I met some of our new immigrants from Estonia the other day," says Willy. "Over a hundred of 'em are hoping to settle in Nova Scotia. Others are headed to Upper Canada and out west, and even more are going down to the States."

"The ones comin' here ... what exactly do they plan on doing for a livin'?" Frank asks the question most of his fellow loafers have in mind. "Do they have any special skills or trades?"

"If you ask me, we don't need no more DPs," says Titus. "Mackenzie King tells us Canada's got a labour shortage. But good payin' jobs are what are needed, there's no shortage of labour. We got enough problems with the Newfoundlanders squeezin' our people out of their jobs. The Liberals got their wires crossed. Last thing we need is more DPs."

"Well, the Newfies are not DPs, and they're awful good fishermen, you got to give 'em that. The ones I've sailed with are big strong men, born to the sea and to fishin' for a livin', you," says Frank.

"Well, that may be, but they're takin' up our jobs. And as cook I can tell you they eat a ton. They're at it all the time ... always after a mug-up. They can't get enough to eat back home. If they're not sleepin' or fishin', or eatin', they're looking for a mug-up. We don't need them, and we don't need no more DPs."

"Aw, they can't be all that bad, Titus," says Willy. "I met some Estonians in Lower Rose Bay the other day, and they seem to be settlin' in pretty good. I met the Liivas, and that family's already lookin' into buyin' a boat. They got two young boys. I met an older fellow from another family too, a young bachelor, name of Wayno or something like to that – the kids speak better English than their parents – but they all seem friendly enough. I know they've built a communal sauna. Guess that's their way of keepin' clean. They don't use bathtubs like us. The families could be related for all I know. Once they make a start, they'll be fine. We can do with some new blood in the community anyway, I reckon."

"Nothing wrong with that," says Austin. "My daughter Virginia was asked if she could try and teach 'em English, anyone who wants to, that is. I think the name of the young man you mentioned, Willy, is Vaino," says Austin, and he slowly spells out the name out to be sure. "Vaino Kariler. He's one of her students."

'Trying to marry her off, are you, Austin?" Frank jokes, but his target pretends not to hear the jibe.

"How come they chose Nova Scotia?' asks Roy. "And where exactly is Estonia anyway?"

"It's in northern Europe, north of Germany … part of the Soviet Union," AB explains. "The country gained its independence in 1918, but the Soviets invaded in 1939. During this last war the Germans took it over and made it part of Germany for a few years. Then, towards the end of the war, the Soviets won it back again as the Germans retreated."

"And they're hanging on to it, I suppose," says Roy.

"Estonia is one of Baltic countries, three of 'em – Estonia, Latvia, and Lithuania," AB elaborates. "Since the war they're all considered part of the Soviet Union. But I expect they'd prefer to be independent. It's a long story, and I can't say I know the half of it, but you can well imagine they've suffered a lot of persecution from invaders over the years. The people coming to Nova Scotia now are looked on as refugees fleeing Soviet domination. They can count themselves fortunate to have been offered sanctuary in Canada."

"The Estonians are probably pretty smart fishermen," says Willy. "Could be they might even teach us a few things. The government's helpin' in the resettlement. There's a couple of families of Estonians over in Feltzen South. They're plannin' to fish herrin'. That's the big thing right now. The price is high. That's what they was doin' over in their country before the Russians chased 'em out. And I know of another family lookin' to start fishin'. I hear they're checkin' over several locations for possible moorings, north of the Pioneer Cemetery. There's that channel dug right in to the shore where Carl Knock's got his wharf. And a house is for sale over near Max and Evelyn Mosher's. They'll do well, you'll see. Don't know what religion they are, but hey, that doesn't matter a whole lot, does it? Long as they're not Roman Catholic."

"They'll find it pretty lonely around here if they are," says Austin.

"Not sure of their affiliation. Probably like Canada, it's a mixed bag back where they come from," says Titus. "Maybe the Presbyterians can take 'em in. Reverend Mawhinny will be happy to have them. He's a new recruit himself."

"Strange name, though," says Austin. "Maybe he's a DP."

"Mawhinney's not a DP, Austin. Come on! He's a genuine immigrant, hardly someone tryin' to sneak in under the wire," Roy puts in.

"The Estonians aren't sneaking in either," says Frank.

"Well, I can tell you for sure, the Rose Bay Estonians are Lutherans," AB tells the gathering. "They've already joined our congregation. That was one of the first things they did after arriving here. They're good people."

"So that answers my question," says Willy. "The young man I was talkin' about earlier, Vaino, he's about my age. He arrived here with his mother and father in mid-June last year, least that's what I understood him to say."

"Vaino? I told you, he's one of the ones Virginia is teaching English to," Austin repeats.

"Vaino and me could understand each other pretty well," says Willy." He told me about the government helpin' him get started. Loaned him five hundred dollars towards buyin' his boat. Helpin' him and his family gettin' a place to stay. I think he said they already have a place a short distance up the road from Max, same side of the road. And when his parents are not knittin' herrin' and mackerel nets for him, they've been puttin' in a garden. Talk about industrious, you, they'll do well!"

"I heard they're good workers," says Frank. "Who knows, we might even learn a few things from 'em."

"I don't know about that," says Titus. "Long as they're not takin' jobs from us."

"Don't you worry about that, Titus. They'll make good citizens. You'll see. Why, Vaino already flies two flags side by side at his place, the Union Jack and the blue, black, and white flag of Estonia. He and his family are happy, and mighty glad to be here."

"Union Jack above the Estonian?" asks Titus.

"Yes, indeed."

"And does he lower the Union Jack at sunset?"

"I'm not sure he does or not."

"Well, he should. The sun should never be allowed to set on the Union Jack."

Remember the Clyde Valley (1951)

"So, Titus, you home for a while?" asks Austin.

"Yeah, a week or so, I'd guess."

"How do you like sailin' on the *Clyde Valley*? I noticed her yesterday when I was down in Riverport."

"Oh, I like it okay," is the response, marked by neither enthusiasm nor elaboration. For once, Austin doesn't follow up with an interrogation.

"It's easier than managing on a schooner, I'd imagine," says Frank, filling in where Austin left off. "Suits WR's purpose too, seein' as he's been buildin' up his fleet the last couple of years. Must have half a dozen or more full-rigged schooners by now, I think. But how come you made the switch from schooners to a steel-hulled motorship, Titus?"

"She was converted from steam to diesel when they brought her to Canada in the early '40s. I been with her for a year or more now. WR's a good man to work for. The *Clyde Valley*'s a bit on the small side, an old ship and slow, but she gets you there – ideal for the home trade. On our usual run we take a load of dry and pickled fish down to the Caribbean and return with salt from Turks Island. This last trip we carried a load of alewives, all packed into barrels. We took 'em on in Halifax – gaspereau I think they call 'em up in the Valley."

"We call 'em kyack around here," says Willy.

"Oh, good evening, Reverend," says AB, as David Mawhinney enters The Shop. The greeting echoes around the pot-bellied stove and is duly acknowledged by the Presbyterian minister. After nearly three years in the community, he is scarcely a stranger.

"Where did you get rid of them?" asks Frank.

"Get rid of what?" asks Titus.

"The gaspereau."

"Haiti. Docked in Port au Prince. There's a big market for them there. When the stevedores take a break I've seen 'em chomp down a salted gaspereau for a snack just like you'd eat an ice cream. Hot as the devil there bytimes."

"Who's the captain of the *Clyde Valley* now?" Austin asks.

"Ross Creaser's been captain ever since WR bought her."

"Do any of you gentlemen happen to know how that ship got her name?" asks Reverend Mawhinney, who is making one of his rare Saturday evening appearances at The Shop. Surprised to hear the Reverend venturing interest in a shipping matter, all hands look up, on alert.

Titus responds, "She's English built, that much I know. More than that I'm afraid I can't tell you."

"Some people might claim her for the Irish, seeing as she was built in my hometown back in Antrim, Northern Ireland. But you're correct, Titus, she's an old English-built ship – a small part of Ireland's history really. She was built by McIlwaine and Lewis in 1886."

"That's well over half a century right there," says Frank.

"Her first name was *Balniel*, after the owner, Lord Balniel, a wealthy Englishman. Swedish steel was used in her construction. Lord Balniel was a fussy man. He insisted that only the best materials be used. So he spared no expense. You see, he was a rich man, the owner of several coal mines in Wales. And for the first twenty-five years or so, until just before World War I, the ship was used as a collier to transport coal and coke between Ireland and Scotland – from several Irish ports over to London, but usually to Glasgow, in Scotland. And it's at Glasgow that the River Clyde flows through the Clyde Valley into the Irish Sea. That's how the *Clyde Valley* got her name."

"There's not a whole lot of intrigue in carrying coal," says AB. "I thought she might have had a more interesting history – with a bit of romance thrown in for good measure somewheres along the line."

"Oh, I don't know about that. I doubt one could call it romantic. There's nothing very romantic about war. But I understand the ship was captured by the Germans and used by them during World War I." Mawhinney pauses as he recalls details of what, for him, is scarcely his normal subject matter.

"How on earth did that come about," Roy asks, "that the Germans got hold of her?"

"The story goes that just before war began, the Orangemen, the Ulstermen hardliners – the Irish in Northern Ireland who favour independence from English rule – somehow managed through the Germans to charter the ship to carry some goods from Germany to Ireland. The shipment would be guns, but of course they didn't say this. This was just before war broke out. I imagine they figured a dirty old nondescript collier wouldn't attract much attention from anyone."

"Were they successful?" asks Willy.

"Yes, I'm sorry to say they were. Due to the constant change of name boards the authorities weren't able to keep track of her. She's said to have made many trips from Germany to Ireland running guns to the Irish Republican Army. You see, in her time, the *Clyde Valley* sailed under a lot of different names." Former rum-runners among the loafers that evening could readily relate to that particular criminal convenience. "Thousands of German rifles," Mawhinney continues, "… no, tens of thousands of rifles, and millions of rounds of ammunition made it through to Irish ports from Hamburg. Finally, in 1916, an English destroyer caught up with the gun-runners and put an end to those activities."

"But you say the Germans got hold of her. How did that happen?" Roy repeats.

"Well, I'm not sure how it happened, but I'd guess the ship was in a German port at the time war broke out. The Germans just took her over and put her to work for them."

"That's very interesting, Reverend. I had no idea of her history," Titus remarks.

"I don't mind telling you folks about it now, but five years ago when my family and I immigrated to Canada, I wouldn't have dared bring up the subject."

"Oh, why's that?"

"Look, you know, the war had just come to end. As a major shipbuilding centre, Belfast and the area all 'round about was the target of heavy bombing by the Germans during the war. The attack on April 15, 1941 – Easter Tuesday – was particularly heavy. And more than once German war planes made strafing runs over our village. A lot of our people, including some close friends, were killed by machine gun fire. Our little house in Templepatrick was completely destroyed by bombs. The only thing salvaged was my wife's piano. Edith had saved up for years to buy it. That was the only thing we brought over to Canada, that and four small wooden boxes with personal items – clothing, wedding gifts, silverware, and books. We arrived on Pier 21 on September 15, 1948, and moved directly to Rose Bay."

"We're glad you made it, Reverend," says Austin.

"Thank you for that," says Mawhinney. "And here we are, coming to a place where most of the people are of German origin. We couldn't believe we were headed to such a community when we had just been bombed out."

"Small wonder, though, that you wanted to make a fresh start," says AB.

"That's true. But look where we ended up. On arrival in mid-September in 1948, we found ourselves in a community settled by Germans. They seemed to speak some English, but even so, we had trouble understanding them. Especially difficult to understand were people from Kingsburg. It took us a long time to get used to things."

"Even here, in Upper Rose Bay, we have trouble understanding the Kingsburgers," says Austin, with a sideways glance towards Titus, who rewards him with a fearsome scowl.

"Apart from all that, there was the food. At Harvest Festival in the church that fall, the people piled all kinds of produce in front of the pulpit for the use of the minister and his family. Pumpkins, squash, carrots … all kinds of garden produce. And other farm produce like pigs-pudding, blood pudding, and the sausages you make here in Lunenburg County – none of that is found in Ireland. I should know, for I used to do the butchering on our family farm back in Templepatrick. We didn't know what to do with the salt cod. And lobsters, I remember the first time a fisherman brought some to the manse as a gift. There he stood, at the door, a big lobster in each hand, waving them around in front of our faces, proud as Punch. My wife, she nearly passed out. We had never seen lobsters before."

"But you settled in well, and we're glad to have you aboard," says Titus, who just happens to have been born Presbyterian. No sooner does he voice this rare compliment than Reverend Mawhinney confesses his latest news.

"Thank you. But I have to tell you that we will be leaving shortly for Montreal."

"Montreal? Why would anyone want to go there?" exclaims Austin.

"Well, you see, I haven't yet been ordained. I'm what, in the Presbyterian Church, is known as a catechist. A catechist is a teacher who provides guidance. An ordained minister, now, is someone who has received his holy orders and has been formally admitted to the ministry."

"It's sort of like a ticket, isn't it?" says Austin, as if he fully understands the Reverend's role in life and society. As for Mawhinney, he's beginning to wonder why he ever embarked on such a complicated mission. Rather than elaborate, he seeks a way out by agreeing with Austin.

"Yes, you see, I feel the call to earn that ticket. And the only way I can do that is to seek ordination. So I'll be working towards that at the Presbyterian College in Montreal starting this fall."

"Do you plan on coming back here after you finish?" asks Titus.

"I'd be glad for an opportunity to return, all in due time. Unfortunately, that decision is not entirely in my hands."

"Guess we'll have to wait and see, and hope for the best. Good to know, though, that you've overcome the problems of livin' here."

"That's true, thank goodness. The Irish have had their share of troubles over the years. Like I was telling you, the *Clyde Valley* is really a part of Irish history – a small but nevertheless significant part. Here now, I'll try to explain for you, best I'm able to, how it's been for the Irish.

"The Act of Union in 1801 made Ireland part of the United Kingdom. Of course, this did nothing to lessen the agitation of those Irish who sought independence, that is to say, home rule. But it satisfied the Unionists who were in favour of British rule – and they haven't changed, especially the Unionist hardliners in the northern province of Ulster."

"Unionists, those would be Protestants – the Orange, right? With Roman Catholics, the Greens, on the other side of the fence," says AB, not really wanting to get too deeply involved in any religious or political controversy. But Reverend Mawhinney, as keen on politics as he is on religion, continues the ride on this merry-go-round of enquiry.

"Correct," he answers. "The Orange Order is a conservative Unionist organization accused of supporting paramilitary groups. It doesn't accept non-Protestant members or Protestants married to Catholics. Nasty incidents happen whenever Orangemen march through Irish Nationalist neighbourhoods."

"Why do they bother making trouble like that?" asks Austin.

"Oh, they like to celebrate an old battle they won over the Catholics – The Battle of the Boyne."

"When was that?"

"That was back in 1690. That's when the English took over and began ruling Ireland."

"When are you leaving anyway?" Austin interrupts undiplomatically.

"The movers are coming next week, I'm afraid. We'll be leaving about the same time, driving up to Montreal in our car. That reminds me, I'd better get on home and help with the packing. I also have to prepare for the service tomorrow. So I'll say *Au revoir*, which I believe means until we meet again. And I really hope that comes about sometime," he adds, making his way out of The Shop.

"Does anybody know who's takin' over from Reverend Mawhinney?" says Austin. "He didn't say."

"I understand they have Daniel MacPherson, but don't ask me where he's from," says AB.

"Well, Titus," says Willy, "I guess you never realized what a historic old tub you've signed on to. Who would have known she was in the gun-runnin' business – before the First World War even!"

"Rum-runnin' too, from what I hear," Frank adds, relaying what seems to be common knowledge in this shaded corner of the Maritime community.

"No way of provin' that of course," says Roy. "But it's no secret she's engaged in bringing up liquor for the Nova Scotia Liquor Commission from the Caribbean. She's been doin' that now for a couple of years, hasn't she, Titus?"

"So I hear tell. I expect WR's been given a license from the government to do that. But that's not rum-runnin'."

"Maybe not, but it's a damn fine cover for someone who might want to bring along a little extra," says Willy.

"Who could that be, I wonder ...?" asks Frank.

"Now I'll tell you something," says AB. "The practice is alive and well. A week ago Friday, I was driving home when a car going much too fast clipped me just as I was about to turn into my yard. The driver didn't stop, but an hour or so later he came back and stopped in to talk with me. He wanted to tidy things up … pay for the damages. Of course, he had been drinking, probably celebrating delivery of another load. The damage could have been a lot worse."

"How do you know he had a load of rum in his car?"

"Why, he admitted as much to me, knowing that nothing much could be done about it at that stage of the game. He'd have cleaned up his car, and who knows where he made the delivery? It could have been any one of a number of bootleggers. Heavens knows there's enough of 'em around. But my wife gave him a royal tongue-lashin.' Carrie's never at a loss for words. He won't forget that for a while."

"There's a lot of young fellas are into it, that I know," says Frank. "The stuff shows up pretty well every time the *Clyde Valley* comes to Riverport."

"How else would Albert Eisenhauer get hold of all that unbonded booze he keeps offerin' around – 150 proof, no tags or seals across the bottle tops. You can be sure Customs has never seen any of that," says Willy.

"That figures. He's still workin' for WR," Carmen says. "WR looks after his own. And Albert is hardly the only one. WR's got a good thing going with the *Clyde Valley*. She's been a money-maker. There's a lot of people workin' the system, wouldn't you say, Titus?"

"I can't rightly say," is his response. But Titus is no innocent, as a peek beneath the stairs leading down into the cellar of his house in Rose Bay would reveal following any given trip on the *Clyde Valley*.

"How does WR do it anyway?" asks Willy. "After all, government inspectors are always present during the unloading of a shipment of booze."

"Who knows?" says Frank. "It's probably no great amount anyway. Nothin' like the old days. A fake bulkhead's easy enough to install, but the *Clyde Valley*'s only got a few cargo holds, and you couldn't hide anything in them. The only place possible might be in the fo'c'sle or perhaps the engine room behind a couple of bulkheads. The Irish gun-runners likely didn't bother building bulkheads. It was all or nothin' with them, I'd imagine."

"Gun-running, rum-running, what's the difference. They're both illegal and only cause trouble," says AB, abandoning any effort to try and moderate this ad hoc forum. Signing off for the evening he can only add: "Who knows what's coming next?"

Tuna Tussle (1952)

"Hello there, young man, how are you making out?" Frank asks Max Mosher, a shore fisherman from Lower Rose Bay.

"Not bad," says Max. "I just thought to drop by and see how you fellas are makin' out. An' I wanted to see Willy here, and see what I can learn about his fishin' tricks."

"Fishin' tricks?" says Willy. "Not much chance I can teach you much of anything. Least not with that old scow you sold me a while back."

"Ha! That was a good boat, and we gave you a good deal on it too. Then you went and changed the name on it after you let it sink. Whatever became of *Watchit* anyway? Sold at a profit, I'd imagine."

In reply, Willy responds with an indignant snort.

"We all heard about the fun you had with that tuna," Titus puts in. "Nothin' stays secret long around here."

"Tuna? What tuna?" says Max, first pretending ignorance, then responding to an urge to share his excitement. "Yes, the tuna have been runnin' strong lately, following the herring. It's been a good year for both."

"So let's have it. Tell us about your big catch," says Willy.

"Get him that chair from the corner," AB tells the gathering. "Come, Max, sit down, man, and make yourself comfortable."

"Well, I was late gettin' out yesterday. I have herrin' nets set out there in Kingsburg Bay. And there was an awful lot of herrin' there. Heavy nets, hard haulin', right full of 'em. And as I was haulin',' once in a while a herrin' falls out of the net, you know. And I seen a great whirl in the water. An' I looked overboard, an' I seen this big fish after the herrin'.

"He grabbed the herrin' and away he went, and I said, Why, that's a tuna. Well, I just happened to have a tuna hook in the boat on one of the old rum kegs. I had about fifty fathom of rope wound on that keg, and on the end of it I had the tuna hook.

"I said, I should try and hook onto that one. So I baited up the hook, put a herrin' on, throwed it overboard, and let it go, oh, about eight feet under the water. And then I tied a ganging on it and made it fast to a marine bolt on the stern of the boat. So that was if he came back again, he would take the hook, and the ganging would snap.

"So I went up to the bow again, and went on haulin' my net. And I wasn't at the bow two minutes when I heard a crack! So, shit! I said, there he is. And I left the net where it was, tied off in the bow, and went back to the stern. He had the keg pulled off the stern of the boat, and it was going Rrrh! Rrrh! Rrrh! Just like you hear when tick-tackin' – like we used to do as kids, with a tick-tackin' spool, an' rubbin' the rosin on a long string to annoy people at Halloween.

"And he took that fifty fathom of rope right out. But I was in a bad spot, you, in among the nets. And it was thick o' fog too. I knew Spinny wasn't far from me. But I didn't call to him then. Only after I got the tuna up by the boat – after a long time."

"How long did it take you?"

"Oh, I'd say maybe half to three quarters of an hour."

"Towing you around all that time?"

"Yeah, well see, when he'd go up near the nets, it wasn't so good. The net is on an anchor of course, and the sonofabitch when he came up, the keg would catch on the rope and the boat was goin' like this – back and forth – he was yanking on it. But he couldn't pull the anchor, you know. That was fast to the bottom. And I'd get him up, and then I'd have to let him go again. But I tried to play him out. I really played him out. Just my bare hands … when I was finished, my hands was like that," says Max, holding his hands first open, revealing the damage, than closing them slowly. "For a while there, I couldn't hardly open them up.

"And there I had him by the side of the boat, and I thought, I can't get this in the boat. So I hollered out in the fog to Spinny. I hollered to him – he wasn't that far from me – but it was thick a' fog, just that I couldn't see him.

"And he said, 'What do you want?'

"And I said, 'I got a tuna here. Come on and help me get it in the boat when you get your net hauled.'

"'Okay,' he said, and he wasn't that long, 'cause I think he had it pretty well hauled. So he come over and got in my boat, and with the two of us on the side of the boat, and this big tuna, she was layin' over like that, you know. So we said, now let's put a rope around its tail."

"Good thing it was calm yesterday," says Willy.

"Oh, it was calm all right, dead calm. So we put a rope around his tail, and one through his gills, and we had him up alongside of the boat. And the boat, she was way down on her side. Now, I said, we'll both pull at the same time, one at the head, and the other at the tail. We rolled the boat back and forth, and as we pulled together, by God, he came right into the boat, on top of the bed boards.

"'Here,' said Spinny, 'how 'bouts we have a little celebration?' So from the stern of his boat he pulls out a bottle of Don Q and, together, we toast my good luck. I have to tell you, it tasted some good!"

"How big, you say?"

"Five hundred and ninety-eight pounds!"

"Dressed?"

"Oh yes, dressed. That's the first one I ever caught in my life. I'll never forget that … never, never, never."

"Guess you can be pretty proud of yourself all right."

"Yes, and I brought it in to shore to the stage to show it off. Then I jumped back in the boat and headed for Lunenburg."

"How much did you get for that tuna?"

"Guess," says Max.

"Oh, ten cents a pound?" says AB, from behind the counter.

"Five cents a pound! Thirty bucks! That's a pretty good day's work I'd say."

"Better than herrin' fishin'," says Roy.

"An old fisherman like you has probably seen some pretty good paydays too," says Max.

"Roy's not old, Max. Only rocks and trees get old. Roy's just been around for a long time," says Willy. "Carl Knock's been doin' pretty well catching tuna too, I hear."

"Yeah, he trolls for 'em. But he's just been catchin' the little ones … tinkers compared to the one I got. Could be he's using smaller hooks. You have to ask him," says Max, getting up and preparing to leave.

"Well, that could be, but I'll bet he's havin' lots of fun doing it."

"Good story," Willy says to Max. "But look, please tell us something before you go. I know you've been responsible for settin' out those navigational buoys in Rose Bay harbour ever since your father passed away. But how come they're changed to a different type now? I liked the old ones better. Those were Styrofoam and they floated high, bobbin' up and down on the water – no trouble at all seein' 'em. But I don't know about these new ones."

"Well, I'll tell you," says Max, sitting down again, "the people in the Department of Fisheries always have bright ideas. Someone decided to change the Styrofoam buoys to large plastic ones, weighing about fifty pounds each, weighted in the bottom with cement. My God, they're heavy. And I agree, they don't work well. I've told 'em so, but of course, they don't listen."

"How many buoys are there out there anyways?" asks Roy.

"There's twenty-two in all. Six buoys are set over the rocky part of the channel. They're the hardest to put in … four red buoys and two green ones. Of course the green ones are on the left-hand side comin' in. The first red one was right on the bar. There's a huge granite boulder the size of this room beside the first green buoy. When I worked with my father during the war we attached the buoys to twelve-foot-long spruce poles. We cut them back in the woods, dragged them home, dried them and painted them, and drilled a hole in the bottom of each for a metal shackle. Then we threaded a rope through each shackle and attached granite rocks to the end to weigh the buoys down. They're set out in the spring, and I remove them in January every year."

"Sounds like a lot of work."

"That was the hardest part for sure. The other sixteen markers were narrower poles stuck into the muddy water bed so that the spruce tops stick out of the water."

"You plan to keep on doin' that job?"

"Well, I've no plans to retire just yet, if that's what you mean. And the Fisheries Department pays me forty dollars a year for doing it."

"You won't get rich doin' that. Better stick to fishin'," says Willy.

"Yes, tuna fishin'!"

"Did you ever get around to fixin' old Bertie's fence?" Frank inquires. "He was in here just the other day complainin' about you. What exactly was it happened?"

"Oh, that. I'm surprised Bertie brought the matter up," says Max. "But you might as well know the truth … clear the air, so to say. John Kaizer wanted to go for a drive, and he wanted company, so he asked me to come with him on a Friday back in mid-September. Normally I wouldn't mind, but I'd been diggin' potatoes all day and I was tired. So I told him, 'No, I'm tired, I'd better say no.' But he insisted, and told me if I'd come he'd let me drive. Well, I thought, that would be good practice for me, 'cause I haven't got my proper driver's license yet."

"So he got you to drive him around?" says Frank.

"Yeah. We went first down to Riverport, and on the way back here's these two girls Dr. Barss has hired to help him – Linda Butts, and I forget the other one's name – walkin' along the side of the road. So John, he tells me to stop, and he says to 'em, hop in if you want a ride. So in they hopped. John told me to drive and he got in the back seat with the girls. 'Let's go to Lunenburg,' he tells me.

"So we went all the way into Lunenburg and back, and I'm feelin' really tired by then. An' all the while he's in the back seat with these girls. I had no idea what was goin' on in the back seat of the car. But see, I was goin' too darn fast. Nobody said nothin' to me. Nobody complained. But I remembered the turn here at the Crossroads and the next thing I heard a racket and saw fence boards flyin' by. It was a section of Bertie's fence that I clipped. Did a good job on it, I guess. Lucky for me, I saw those two big trees out front of his place just in time, and managed to miss 'em. Only one fender damaged. John, he didn't mind. 'That's easy fixed,' he said.

"Of course, when my father heard about it, he told me, 'You'll be hearing from Bertie about this.' And he was right. Bertie let him know the next day that his fence was broken and that Max has to fix it. 'I'll say nothing about it if he fixes it,' he told my father. But Bertie owes money for groceries that he got some time back from my father's store – it's right across the road from our place, you know. He's a jeezly old bugger, is Bertie. So my father, he told him, 'Now I'll tell you something, Bertie, when you pay up your grocery bill, I'll see you get your fence fixed up.' And that was the end of that. We haven't heard from him since."

"Here he comes now," says Austin, at which Max jumps up and makes for the exit.

"Just kidding," says Austin with a laugh.

Out at the Ice (1955)

"Well, hello there, captain. It's been a while since we've seen you around these parts. You been fishing?" AB asks, as the imposing stalwart figure of Douglas Himmelman enters The Shop.

"Good evening all. No, I'm trying something new. I'm a pilot now – nautical, not flying. Got my papers a month or so ago, and I'm working out of Halifax. Thought I'd drop by and say hello. I've just been out to Gladee's Canteen for supper. It's a bit of a squeeze fitting everyone into that Sea Breeze, but oh, the food and friendly reception make it all worthwhile."

"I'm glad to hear she's doin' well. This is the third, or is it the fourth year, since Gladee started the canteen," says AB.

"The Hirtles are hard workers."

"Sounds like you're makin' a big switch, Douglas."

"Yes, I am. But piloting is a good job. I got lucky. I meet a lot of people, keep up with the shipping news, and," pausing for emphasis, "I get home a lot more than I ever did fishing or coasting. If I stick with it, I'll get pensioned off in the end, which is more than my poor old father could ever say."

"Tommy Alonzo, yes, I remember you sailed with your father on the old *Bessemer* during the war, didn't you?" says Roy, old man of the sea.

"That was in 1939, for a year or so after I turned seventeen. Titus was cook with us. Do you remember, Titus? And a damn good cook he is too. How are you, Titus? I remember my father and I made a special trip down here to Rose Bay to get you signed on. You couldn't fill a man up in those days. Titus made a big friggin' mincemeat turnover on my seventeenth birthday that trip. It was like half a pie! I still have a picture of it somewhere."

"Yeah, I remember," says Titus.

"Funny thing about the *Bessemer*. My father had her built in 1927, and all four of his sons – every one of us under ten years – me, and my brothers Bruce, Donald, and Edgar, we all got scarlet fever. Bruce Malcolm and Donald Arthur died of it, but Father had already named the vessel *Donald and Bruce*. When they died, he took the name board off the vessel, turned it upside down, and burned the name of the ship's auxiliary engine, *Bessemer*, on the other side. Like I said, I sailed on the *Bessemer* with my father to the Banks in 1939. Several years later she was sold off in Newfoundland. I'm not sure what happened to her after that – perhaps her name was changed, or maybe she was lost. I'm not sure. Anyways, my father told me that years later her name board was found on a beach off the south coast of Newfoundland."

"That name board's got quite a history. Should be in a museum somewhere," says Austin. "I remember you tellin' us about tryin' to cook spaghetti on the engine of that Lunenburg rum-runner. What was the name again?"

"You must mean the *Mudathalapadu*. Well, I didn't really sail on her, you know."

"I remember seein' the *Mudathalapadu* in Lunenburg oncest," says Frank.

"Might have been the year you blew up the can of spaghetti, Doug," says Carmen. "Robert Cook told me they had a run-in with the American Coast Guard 'round about that time. He said he was busy doin' some maintenance work on the engine. They were away down in international waters off Boston.

But a cutter spotted them and began to harass them. The cutter steamed 'round and 'round the *Mudathalapadu* an' usin' their fire hose sprayed them with bilge water and black paint."

"That wasn't very nice of them," says Austin, having little idea of the dirty tricks played by both sides during the rum war.

"No, it wasn't, but what was even worse, Robert told me the cutter threw a grapnel over the rum-runner's wireless aerial, tearing it down. That prevented ship-to-shore contact being made. The thing is," Frank continues, "according to Rob they was all ready to make a high-speed run ashore to discharge their cargo. Likely the Coast Guard guessed as much, for the rum-runner would have been settin' low in the water."

"How did they make out at the end of it?"

"Rob said they did it. He got the engine workin' again and, runnin' at top speed with their smokescreen turned on, they lost the cutter and made their drop. Mission accomplished. That sort of thing happened fairly often."

"That's a good story," Douglas admits with a smile. "Sorry I missed out on the adventure. I was only a teenager at the time. After the *Bessemer*, I sailed on the *Passadena*, before joining the merchant navy during the war. Made quite a few trips on ships of the Park Steamship company, all of them freighters built for the merchant navy during the war. I suppose they were the equivalent of the American Liberty Ships. There was three or four of them … the *Lisbon Park*, *Mount Royal* … all built up in Sorel, Quebec.

"One of the first ones I sailed on was the *Dufferin Park*, mostly on trips to South America. And although we escaped attack by U-Boats we suffered all the same. We slept with our life jackets on. I made too many trips on the *Dufferin Park*. She was a 4,700-ton freighter built up in Quebec. She didn't have a very good reputation – 'sufferin' on the *Dufferin*' we used to say."

"How come she had such a bad reputation?" Austin asks.

"The *Dufferin* was what you'd call a sad ship. We had so

many different nationalities on board as crew … English people from all over the place, black fellas from the Caribbean, Czechoslovakians, South Americans. So that's where the sufferin' on the *Dufferin* started. She was not a happy ship, so you suffered more than you were happy. The captain was German – C.J.R. Kohler, Carl Kohler, was master. The mate on the *Dufferin* was Danish, there was a French Canadian second mate, and the third mate might have been Czechoslovakian … I forget his name. We had crew changes all the time."

"How could you be sailing on a Park ship with a German captain during the war?" asks AB.

"It's a long story. Carl Kohler, you must ha' all heard of him. He was born at sea on a German ship named *Carl*. But after that he became a naturalized Canadian citizen. He lived in Lunenburg, just up the street from the foundry … on the other side, where the Bluenose Lodge is now. I made my first trip with old Carl on the *John Cabot*. Nobody liked him very much. He was a strange fellow. He used to sleep with a revolver under his pillow. But I was just a sailor. By the end of the war he was a famous guy – was awarded the OBE, the Order of the British Empire."

"What did he do to deserve that?" Austin asks.

"I'm not sure of the details, but I think he set sail in the *John Cabot* and landed in Nazaire, France, in 1940, on the very day it capitulated to the Germans. Then, against orders from the French Vichy government, he set sail despite constant bombing, evaded a German blockade, and made for England, where he delivered an important cargo of wood used to make plywood to manufacture Mosquito airplanes.

"I sailed with Carl's son Henry too. We became good friends. He married my cousin Evangeline Himmelman. They live out on the east end of Lunenburg, just above the shipyards. I remember once back in 1942 we went together to sign on with the *Liverpool Loyalist*. The first mate was a fellow from Montreal, named Meldrum. His ship, the *Vinland*, had just been torpedoed. We heard they were hiring, and the bosun told us to go and report to the chief mate. So we did. We went and rapped on his door. 'Come in!' he roared. 'Give me your names.' 'Douglas Himmelman and Henry Kohler,' says Henry. 'Christ! Are you the bastards who sank the *Vinland*?'"

After the knowing chuckles among the loafers die down, Douglas continues without pause.

"Then after the war I sailed on the *Mount Royal Park*. Captain A.B. Tanner was the master. We carried wine from France to various countries. You could drink the stuff, but we didn't like it. Murray Himmelman, the chief engineer, he helped us build a still. We distilled the wine. Out of seven gallons of wine you could get one gallon of pure alcohol. After that, I smartened up and studied for navigation. Got my Masters certificate in 1950, I believe it was."

"Good thing too," mutters AB under his breath.

"What did you do then?" asks Austin.

"No jobs in sailin' anymore, sailin' ships are goin' out of style. So I went coasting on freighters that sailed between the Eastern Arctic and the Gulf of St. Lawrence. It's a long story, and we could be here all night. Oh, and I also spent several seasons sealing off Newfoundland on the *Arctic Sealer* ... don't know that you ever heard of her ...?"

Douglas, though born in Riverport in 1923, was brought up in the house opposite the Presbyterian manse along the Rose Bay-Riverport road. He relaxes in the familiar setting of The Shop. A tall husky man, his muscled lively presence is such as would fill the place even in the absence of the six loafers present. He takes his time lighting his pipe.

Watching Douglas settle in, Titus is reminded of Whipper Billy Watson, a wrestler in whom he takes a special delight in watching on the television set he and his wife recently acquired. Titus remembers the day Captain Thomas Alonzo Himmelman and his teenage son arrived at his home to persuade him to join as cook on the *Bessemer*. World War II had been raging for nearly a year then, and his third child, a boy, had been born, just before it all began. On board the *Bessemer,* he recalled being impressed at the sheer enthusiasm of young Douglas for everything nautical, including the "gritty labours of dorymen."

The man before him now, Titus thinks to himself, is not one to suffer fools gladly. Himmelman captains – and there were a great many of them – were known as no-nonsense blue water captains. But he never sailed with old Captain Bertie. That fellow is a law unto himself, Titus reflects, unconsciously contemplating the class distinction between captains and ordinary seamen – I scarcely know Bertie, he thinks, even though the man lives next door to The Shop. Wouldn't be surprised if old Bertie and Douglas are related … yes, of course, Bertie is Douglas's uncle, brother of Tommy.

"My wife Thursa," says Frank, breaking in on Titus's muddled thoughts, "she's from Newfoundland, and she tells me that early on in that business, hundreds of ships took men on what they called ice huntin'. That's what they called it. But she lost some family members on the hunt, and refuses to talk much about it."

"That would ha' likely been immediately before the First World War," says Douglas. "By far 1914 was the worst year. The *Southern Cross* disappeared with all of two hundred and fifty men during a winter storm. And in that same storm, seventy or more sealers were left to freeze to death on the ice. No, it's not a pretty picture at all."

"Tell us what it's really like sealing," Frank says.

"I made three trips to the ice on the *Arctic Sealer*. Last one was in '54. She was a ship that Shaw Steamship Company bought from the Americans after the war – 1949, it was. She was big – about two hundred feet, and had good speed, twelve knots or so. Murray Himmelman was the engineer. They, the sealing crew, would come aboard from all over Newfoundland – St. John's, Twillingate, Corner Book, you name it. We had the ship all cleaned up during the year, but down there at the ice … we'd have eighty men down below half the time and they made an unholy mess of the ship by the time we got back."

"Was there no way to keep it clean?" asks Willie.

"No! No! No! When you get that many men below decks you couldn't do much. They used it like a pigs' pen. The ice captain was the man in charge of the sealers and he appointed quartermasters to supervise groups of twenty men each out of the eighty-man total. I had just a skeleton crew to operate the ship – myself, the cook, the steward, engineer, chief mate, and a half-dozen or so able seamen. The Arctic season for sealing starts in the spring. We'd go the first of March for five or six weeks in the ice, from St. John's. One year, we had a really good trip, going on the number of pelts we got – a lot of bloody ice. We were high-liner in 1953. But truth be known, I really didn't have much to do with the high-lining, because I didn't go on the ice. Yes, yes, I was like the handle on the teapot – I was on it but not in it."

"How did you do as high-liner on your best trip to the ice?" asks Willy.

"Oh, about twenty-five to thirty thousand skins. Took 'em into St. John's. Joe Brothers was our agent. And they'd buy the skins and sell them. I don't know what they did with 'em. There was the *Arctic Sealer*, *Arctic Prowler*, and then four or five Newfoundland ships, so five or six ships altogether. Gilbert Mossman, over in Riverport, was mate with me on one trip. Shaw Steamship, they have an office down on Barrington Street in Halifax. Well, they are heavily involved in shipping. They have ships going to the Caribbean and all over. Alf Shaw is the president. He lives down on Jubilee Road in Halifax. It's big business, but all pretty straightforward stuff – I mean to say, no great adventure."

"You never lost anybody?"

"No, we never lost anybody."

"That's amazing."

"We had a few fellows fall in the water, but we never lost anybody. But you can have your sealing. I liked the summer work best. In the summer we sailed the *Arctic Sealer* out of Saint John, New Brunswick. She was chartered by the Military and Transport Department. We carried people and cargo up the coast to sites along the Pinetree Line – St. Anthony, Cartwright, Hopedale, and on up to DEW Line sites at Resolute and Frobisher Bay. All kinds of equipment we carried: tools, building materials, bulldozers, rock crushers, housing modules, radar equipment, and tons of electronic gear.

"Frobisher Bay, now that's a lively place. When I was up there last year and this, there were a lot of Americans around. They were working hard on the DEW Line, that's the distant early warning radar system, see. It's supposed to help protect us from a sneak nuclear attack over the Pole – by the Soviet Union. The DEW Line was an even bigger project than Pinetree Line.

"Yes, it was in the summertime we did this. In case you're wondering, Canada joined forces with the Americans to establish the Pinetree sites in the early 1950s in Canadian provinces and territories, and these – all forty radar sites – were operational by 1954. The Americans had already started by then on the DEW Line. Those sites run all across the top of the world, from Alaska to Baffin Island. I don't know how many there are – a lot.

"I don't much like sealing. But I enjoyed the rest of my year on the *Arctic Sealer*, running up North. I made friends with different people in towns like St. Anthony and Cartwright. On the mainland there aren't very many towns with any people in them. There wasn't much in Sagalek Bay or in Resolute. I had my wife with me on one trip when we went to Hopedale, and we went to a dance. They had a dance in the community hall. And there was somebody there with a pair of socks that looked exactly like a pair that I owned. Funny, the things you remember. My wife was sure that they were my socks."

"So now you've changed jobs?" AB asks.

"Yes, I was bringing *Arctic Sealer* into Halifax, and my cousin, Carl Himmelman, he asked me if I'm interested in becoming a pilot. Well, of course I said yes. That's a great job, and I'd be working with ships every day. So I went to work and studied up on it – Carl more or less taught me, and took me out on the pilot boat and all things like that. I finished my exam last year. Eleven started the course, seven of us wrote the exam. I was second out of the seven. So I got the second job. I was on a ship taking pulp up to Seven Islands when I got the call to come home and start piloting."

"Congratulations, Douglas!" says AB, to which a mumbled chorus of accord makes its way 'round the pot-bellied stove.

"But it all goes to show you how the old ways are fast changing," says Roy, ever the philosopher sailor. "There's hardly a full sail of canvas to be seen around here anymore."

"Not many fish either," says Frank.

"No, but we got a new hospital. The Fishermen's Memorial is a pretty smart-looking place. Just opened for business," says Willy.

"All at the cost of the Marine Hospital up there on the hill by the Garden Lots. It closed down in March '53, I believe. But it's been a godsend for us fishermen all these years. We will miss it. It's not a big place, less than a dozen beds. But a man was looked after mighty good up there."

"You're right. I been there several times over the years," says Roy, "and they always made a fellow feel right at home. The rooms are small and they all had different names. In the big living room, you could see everything goin' on in the shipyard and the docks."

"What were you in for?" asks Willy.

"The usual," Roy answers, "infected feet from livin' in rubber boots weeks at a time, and blistered hands from handlin' salt, saltwater-infected cuts and sea boils. But they took care of all sorts of problems, like a regular hospital, I'd guess. Reginald Melanson was caretaker and did some of the nursing when I was last there. His wife did a lot of the cookin'."

"During the war it was generally full up … all beds occupied. Patients of all nationalities were accepted. They used to have a parrot when Sid Miller was superintendent. I remember it had a mighty strange vocabulary," says Frank.

"Not surprising is it, with all them foreigners around," says Austin.

"Didn't matter what you got – flu, blood-poisoning, broken bones, Dr. Creighton saw to it that you got taken care of good and proper, and no time wasted. He did minor surgery right there. The more complicated stuff he done at the Dawson Memorial. I know of one man, who was in for seawater boils in '51, spent a whole week there to get his boils looked after. The cost was paid in full under the National Health and Welfare. Long as the ship paid sick mariner's dues, and the patient had papers signed by the ship's captain. It was all paid for out of the Fisherman's Fund, only you had to make sure to see Dr. Creighton first thing."

"On the CB, if they heard a man's comin' ashore with a broken leg, why, Dr. Creighton would be right there on the wharf himself to meet him. Straight to the Marine Hospital they'd go. Dr. Creighton, he was the Marine doctor. But the thing is, if you wanted your bill paid, you had to go straight to him. That's the fella you had to go to first," explains Frank. "The government had nothin' to do with it. The money all come out of the Fisherman's Fund."

"Times are changing, boys," says Douglas, who'd been listening quietly for a time. "We all have to try and make the best of it."

End of an Era (Early November, 1957)

"Now that we have a new federal government, we can expect things to start to happen," says Titus to his fellow loafers. "It took Diefenbaker a while to get where he is, but he's a born fighter. For him and the PCs it's been a thirty-year battle."

"Well, we finally got our road paved – all the way to Lower Kingsburg," says Austin.

"You can thank Bob Stanfield for that. Diefenbaker had nothing to do with it," says AB.

"It don't hurt none to have the PCs in charge at both provincial and federal levels now, does it?" says Titus. "The party here was in pretty poor shape before Stanfield showed up."

"Well, all I'll say is, we did our best to push him over the top."

"How do you mean, 'we'?" Austin asks William.

"In the lead-up to the election, a group of us spent a couple of evenings down at Wentzell's place bottling gifts for all those important undecided voters."

"It paid off," says Titus.

"Who supplied the juice?" Austin asks.

"Why, Shillelagh of course. He's into everything."

"Stanfield's majority win last year was the first in ... must be near twenty years, if not more," says Willy.

"For Diefenbaker, this was his third national election."

"Third time lucky, they say. He must want the job pretty bad."

"He's from Saskatchewan, ain't he?" says Austin.

"Yes, second generation in Canada. His father was the son of German immigrants. But they say Diefenbaker was born in a small town in Ontario. His family moved west when he was little," says AB.

"Well, he's a big man now," says Frank. "He's been gettin' a royal welcome everywhere he goes. Huge crowds turnin' out to see him. People knockin' themselves out just to kiss his coattails. Imagine that! Guess they like what he tells 'em. Let's hope he delivers on some of those promises he's been makin'."

"Oh, he will, he will," says Titus. "Give the man time."

"He's got his job cut out for him. It's quite a list of goodies he's come up with."

"Lower taxes is one thing promised. That shouldn't be too hard to swing. Put me in charge, and they'd be lowered by to-morrow morning," says Austin.

"Tax cuts and an increase in old age pensions is also in the works – same with increased aid to the poorer provinces. Dief wants to promote the welfare of the average man, at least that's what he says."

"Not sure you qualify, Austin," says Willy.

"Don't you go worrying 'bout me. Only see you don't throw away your vote next time."

"I voted right this time 'round," answers Willy. "Diefenbaker says 'Canada first!' He promises to put Canada first in everything he undertakes. I'm okay with that."

"In these times, that's a tall order right there, you," says Frank.

"Talk about a royal welcome," says AB from behind the counter. "Did you know the Queen and Prince Philip were in Ottawa earlier this week where they met up with Diefenbaker? The Queen, she opened Parliament. An' that's another first. She is the first Canadian monarch to open an annual session of the Canadian Parliament."

"That was on Monday, October 14, wasn't it?" says William.

"There's a first time for everything. You ought to know," says Willy. "Did they invite you up to Ottawa to help celebrate the occasion? If they didn't, they should have, seein' as how you helped feed the whole crowd of 'em."

"How's that? What are you talking about?" asks Austin, who evidently has yet to learn of Captain William Leary's catch of a large Atlantic sturgeon.

AB, as usual, up-to-date on political developments, as on general news items, explains to Austin. "Haven't you heard? Captain William here landed a big sturgeon a week or so ago. Now that's a royal fish, and so any sturgeon caught in our waters is automatically the property of royalty. It's an old British tradition. England's Queen is our Queen too, and seein' as she and Prince Philip are in Ottawa right now ..."

"Living high on the hog, thanks to her generous hosts," Willy interrupts.

"Nonsense! Please let me finish, Willy. Austin, can it be that you haven't heard about William and his crew on the *Linda-Jane,* catching that sturgeon off LaHave Islands? Here, you tell us about it, William, I wasn't there. We'd all like to hear the story. It's not every day a record fish is landed around here, let alone a prize like the one you brought ashore."

"It was a fine big fish, that's for sure," answers William. "But I'm afraid there's not much to the story about how it was caught. Trawling's like that, pretty straightforward. Set out the long line and haul it half a day or so later. Still, it surprised me how lively it was when we got it up to the boat.

Crew members aboard the *Linda-Jane* in Lunenburg celebrate their catch of a large sturgeon. Front row, right to left: the cook (unidentified), Captain Charles William Leary, Art Skinner. Back row: Harry Creaser, Dan Skinner, Martin Picco, three unidentified.

"When we came in, Lloyd Crouse, our MP for Queens-Lunenburg, no sooner heard about it than he right away arranged for it to be shipped up to Ottawa for the Queen. He owns a couple of boats, see, including the *Linda-Jane*. 'The Queen has to eat something while she's in Ottawa,' he said, 'so it might just as well be this sturgeon.' This was all news to me. But the crew and I agreed it was the right thing to do. There was more than enough to go 'round at the banquet. We was told it's the Queen's fish really, and seein' as she was in Ottawa on important business, it seemed to us the all 'round appropriate thing to do. Me and the crew consider it an honour. It was right smart of Mr. Crouse to think of doin' that. And he's the man on the spot. He just happened to be in Ottawa at the time. And even though he's a freshman MP, he gets things done."

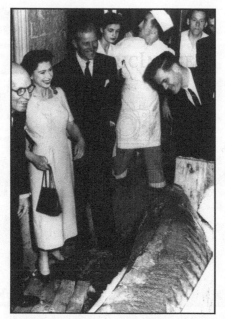

Queen Elizabeth, Prince Philip, and Governor General Vincent Massey (at left) enjoy the sight of a huge sturgeon caught off Nova Scotia as it is presented to the Queen by Lloyd Crouse (at right), MP for Queens-Lunenburg. A cook in charge of preparing the sturgeon for the state dinner hovers in the background. October 13, 1957. United Press International (with permission).

"Lloyd Crouse is a good man. We're lucky to have someone like him in politics to stand up for us. You did the right thing," says Titus.

"It's a good thing," says Roy, "but it's only fair to say that Crouse replaces another good man in Robert Winters. Too bad about Bob Winters in a way. He's a real smart fellow. He just teamed up with the wrong party. His father, Henry, was a sea captain, you know."

"Winters' timing was off. He's gone along with St. Laurent. Good riddance, I say. Never thought we'd see the last of St. Laurent."

"J.J. Kinley's father was also a captain," Roy reminds the company.

"John James, yes, and look at all that man's done," says AB. "Started Kinley's Drug Store, was president of the Lunenburg Foundry, served in both world wars. Why, he was awarded the Distinguished Service Medal by King Haakon of Norway at the end of the Second World War. And that's all beside his leading role in provincial politics during the last few decades."

"Humpf! Another long-time Liberal less," Titus growls.

"We've had more than enough of them," says Roy.

"I'd call it an infestation," Austin volunteers, not to be left out of the PC majority opinion poll among this group of loafers.

"Now that's a bit much, Austin," AB admonishes from his vantage point behind the counter.

"We've been overdue for a change," says Titus, with close to an open smile. His joy of the PCs' jubilant yet precarious position of power subsides just as a latecomer enters.

"Hey there, it's Max Mosher, the marker buoy man. What brings you here?" asks Willy, as Max gets his bearings.

"Good evening all. I heard somebody caught a big fish." Then, spotting William, he asks, "Or am I too late to hear an account from the captain himself? Up at your place, they said I'd probably find you here."

"No, you've come at a good time, Max. We're all done with politics here, aren't we, AB?"

AB shrugs good-naturedly as Max asks, "Tell us, captain, was it male or a female?"

"Female. A big soaker."

"Male or female, it doesn't matter, Max, that sturgeon's long gone. It's a fish reserved for royalty, by law," says Frank. "Tell him how it is, AB, so he doesn't get his hopes up."

"Aw, news gets around. I heard our MP stepped in and had it sent up to Ottawa for the Queen," says Max. "That won't hurt our reputation none. Good job. But I'd like to hear the fishin' story."

"Well, there's not a whole lot to tell. We was trawlin' down off LaHave bank and we knew straight away there was something big on the line. And sure enough, up comes this huge sturgeon. Pretty lively too ... more so than a swordfish or any shark, except maybe for threshers. We was scared it might break free and we'd lose it, but all went well ... got her in close enough to knock on the head, gaff, and hoist on board. Took the guts out of it at sea to help keep it fresh as possible.

"After the weigh-in at the Acadia Fisheries Plant, the plant manager, Tony Wilberham, he right away called up Lloyd Crouse. Crouse was up in Ottawa at the time, so he was able to make things happen. He suggested delivering the sturgeon to the Queen. Mind you, this was on the very same day she arrived in Ottawa – the thirteenth of October."

"That was generous of him," says Austin.

Ignoring Austin's slightly sarcastic comment, William continues, "Lloyd wasted no time in arranging transport for it. An RCAF plane was carrying Premier Stanfield and the Lieutenant Governor Alistair Fraser to Ottawa for the state dinner. So a special stopover in Amherst was arranged to get the fish on board. It wasn't the easiest thing to get into the plane. See, it was packed in ice inside a big wooden crate. Most of the seats had to be removed from the cabin. Apparently the Lieutenant Governor spent the rest of the trip perched on the end of the container.

"After landing in Ottawa, the fish was rushed from Rockcliffe Airport straight to Government House. The Queen had already heard about this gift, and they tell us it was her request that they serve it up on the evening of the state banquet at Rideau Hall."

"You mean to say they ate the whole thing at one go?" Austin asks.

"No, Lloyd said only about fifty pounds were used at the state dinner. Don't worry, Austin, it's not too likely anyone went hungry."

"What became of the rest of it?"

"Good question, Austin. I was told the rest was divided up among the Protestant and Catholic orphanages in Ottawa."

"Nice touch," says AB. "I shouldn't be surprised if the Queen made that request too."

"What did you do with the caviar, William?"

"You know, Max, that's the first thing they asked me when we got to Lunenburg. I had to ask, 'What's caviar?' See, we don't ever keep fish eggs or roe. I know, I know, some people eat the tomalley and eggs of lobsters."

"Yuk," says Austin.

"I heard caviar goes even better with rum than it does with vodka," says Max.

"There must ha' been a barrel of that stuff into it ... caviar or whatever you want to call it. We just 'over the side' with the lot of it."

"Oh my! Oh my," says Max, cradling his head in his hands.

"Wonder if the Queen or Prince Philip asked Crouse about the caviar," says Austin. "I saw their picture with the fish, in *The Chronicle Herald*, and they looked pretty pleased with themselves. The Queen sure is a beautiful-lookin' woman."

"We gotta hope they didn't ask about the caviar," says AB.

"Lloyd said Prince Philip asked him whether we caught many sturgeon. And I think Lloyd told him, no, this was the only one any of our boats had ever caught."

"Don't know about that. Carl Knock gets the odd small one in his gill nets from time to time, and I'm pretty sure he doesn't throw 'em away," says Max.

"So how's the fishin' been down your way?" William asks.

"Oh, there was a fair run of mackerel earlier this fall. And Carmen Knock has been gettin' a few salmon. He fishes gill nets. Not much goin' by way of groundfish. I have to be thinkin' about takin' out the marker buoys fairly soon. Before you know it, lobster season will be startin' up, and then it might be too late. I got traps of my own to look after. No shortage of things to do ... Oh, and did you hear about Vaino?"

"What about Vaino?" Willy asks. "Did he get a new boat?"

"No, he's goin' to get married," says Max.

"Who's he marrying?"

"Pauline Zinck. She used to work in Rissers' Store ... lived with Bernard and Mabel years ago. Vaino and his parents have always been the very best of neighbours. And Vaino's a first-rate fisherman. Looks like a good match. He and Pauline seem to get along together pretty well."

"Well, good for them," sounds a general approval.

"When is it happenin'?" someone asks.

"Pauline, she doesn't want to rush into things none. Neither of 'em does. Vaino says a wedding is in the works, though I can't say as I know exactly when."

"Seems like there's been an awful lot goin' on lately," says Willy to no one in particular, as AB makes ready to close shop. "What else is new, do you suppose?"

"Any of you fellas seen this Soviet *Sputnik* satellite flyin' overhead? That's certainly somethin' new," says Frank. "It was launched way back in early October ..."

"The fourth of October," AB supplies the date as he locks the till. The loafers realize time's up. Someone knocks out a pipe in the coal scuttle. Coats are retrieved from chair backs.

"They said on the radio you could see it on a clear night with the naked eye. So I took a look-see from my back yard about ten o'clock last night. And sure enough, there's this speck of light high in the southwest, like a star, except it's movin' across the sky at a pretty good clip. You should be able to see it again tonight, if it hasn't clouded over."

"It's got the attention of the Americans – they like to think of themselves as the only superpower. They never imagined the Soviets would get into space before they did. Who knows, next thing they'll be in a race to see who first gets a man up there flying 'round the world. There's already been some talk about that," says AB.

"What good would that do? We already have one of those things up there. It's way bigger than a speck in the sky, it's like a big arrow – they call it the Avro Arrow."

"Come on, Austin, the Avro Arrow is a jet plane. *Sputnik*'s a satellite – they're completely different things," says Frank, as he moves toward the door.

"Austin knows better, he's just pullin' your leg," says AB, coming to Austin's rescue. "But you know, it's somethin' of a coincidence that *Sputnik* was launched into space on the very same day the Avro Arrow was introduced to the Canadian public."

"Maybe Diefenbaker ordered it built."

"The Avro Arrow? Not a chance. I doubt very much if he knows it exists or will even care much about it when he does find out," answers AB, prophetically as matters turn out. "He's a politician, and he'll be busy celebrating his big win for at least the next several months. And let's not forget, he's got a minority government to deal with. The PCs only got 112 seats compared to the Liberals 105."

AB closes up, and the loafers call it a night, unperturbed by the news of many changes so swiftly introduced into livelihoods and their down-home country lives. Though their practiced disciplines and expectations are challenged by events beyond their control, they roll with the punches in a political age. They are reconciled to the transitory nature of things, as to the weather.

* * * * *

A new world abuilding even as stargazers look up in helpless wonder. Stardust above, throughout the constellations, and stardust below, walking the earth. Roy and Titus are in a thoughtful mood as they leave the lowering campfire of congeniality in The Shop and head home. It's impossible to escape the weight of history. And their view of things to come is as shapeless as the ocean's roar in the hollow of a seashell. They will continue to make what they can of life's offerings, expecting no more reward than the satisfaction of accepted responsibilities and a sense of belonging. Light years away, the stars, shining lies, wink unintentionally and time stands still as the two men pause at the top of the hill and look up.

"Talk about the changin' times. It's hard to keep up," Roy remarks to his neighbour. "Guess there's some things old fellers like us will never quite understand."

"You mean many things."

"Yeah, many things."

"Fishin's all right, if you like workin' on the new trawlers, but it's nothin' like what it used to be. Satellites up there flyin' over the earth an' TVs takin' over at home."

"Pretty soon there won't be much left for us to do. Just sit back and watch wrasslin'. A feller could get used to that, you know."

"Don't know 'bout that," says Titus. "Least we can do is keep on votin' the right people in."

"We just have to keep on not knowin'. It's hard to tell what's comin' next."

"Trouble is, we're neither of us half-high educated enough to make a go at anything new."

"That's generally the way of things around here. Some things never change. Anyways, we're still here to cheer once in a while when things go right."

"For a change."

"There's that word again."

"Like elections."

"And weddings."

"That too. And by the way, Letoile told me the other day Pauline's had a change of heart."

"Oh, how so?"

"She says she's able now to forgive those who were unkind to her."

"Forgive and forget? Well, that's the way it's got to be, I reckon. I'm right glad to hear it."

"She and Vaino should make out good together."

"No one ever dies of love around here, do they?"

"She didn't name names."

"We don't hardly need to know, do we?"

"What would be the point? We don't need to know everything."

"Wouldn't do no good at all."

Epilogue

Following a fire in The Shop and consequent extensive smoke damage, Arthur Benjamin Lohnes called it quits in early 1958, after nearly four decades of dedicated storekeeping. He passed away at age ninety-eight on May 14, 1985.

Rev. Donald Himmelman, son of Captain William Himmelman, delivered the eulogy – like many memories, since lost and gone forever – shortly before his own tragic passing. AB's wife, Carrie Lenora, died five years later, age ninety-nine.

Pauline's traumatic childhood, succeeded by a bitter betrayal in love, left its mark on her. A young unwed mother, she was welcomed into the household of a kind and generous family. Cautious respect – even fear – of strangers remained with her. Yet she maintained a genuine outgoing sociable nature as well as a sense of humour and this led to her forming close life-long friends in the community. She could express strong feelings, but could accept another point of view. A kind and generous spirit served as guarantee for her forgiving nature.

A slow and steady courtship by respected Estonian immigrant fisherman Vaino Kariler culminated in their quiet marriage in December 1958. Fishing – an integral theme in Pauline's own background – helps sustain several families in the community of Rose Bay, including that of their son

Jaan, despite the drastic global downturn and changes in the industry.

Pauline Marjorie Kariler passed away on January 14, 2018, at the age of eighty-seven, preceded by her husband, Vaino, nearly two years earlier. Devoted in their religion, they enjoyed a happy and fulfilling life together of nearly sixty years. Pauline cherished that life and all her family members to the end. Theirs was a contract that might merit the envy of many newlyweds – a buoyant spirit shines through the poem she selected as centrepiece of the memorial service held for her beloved husband on March 12, 2016.

> *God grant that I may live to fish*
> *Until my dying day*
> *And when it comes to my last cast*
> *Then I most humbly pray*
> *When in the Lord's great landing net*
> *I'm peacefully asleep*
> *That in His mercy*
> *I be judged as good enough to keep.*

Acknowledgements

Many thanks to my publisher, Lesley Choyce, editors Peggy Amirault and Julia Swan, and to graphic artist Gail LeBlanc for their expertise and deft dealing with these rough "down home" Nova Scotia rum tales. Constructive critiques of an early draft of the manuscript were provided by my daughter Andrea and by Margaret Jean Layng, as was proofreading of specific chapters by Ralph Getson and David Laurence Mawhinney.

I would like to thank the many other people who helped me along the way, including my wife Marie, son Kaspar, Susan Crouse, John and Louise Leary, Elaine Ernst, Blanche Mossman, Carol Anne and Monty Mosher, Max Mosher, Donald and Merlene (Creaser) Gerhardt, David Mosher, Pauline Kariler, Jaan Kariler, Melanie Uhlman, Louise and Grevel Acker, Roy and Letoile Deal, Mike Zinck, Bob and Beatrice Zinck, Romaine and Lorna Jane (Romkey) Cook, Sheila Ritcey, Linda (Ritcey) Tolman, Philip Hartling and Gary Shutlak (Public Archives of Nova Scotia), staff at the Acadia University Library – Pat Townsend, Ann Smith, Anthony Pash, Wendy Robichaud, Mike Beazley, Valerie Kneen-Teed, Joseph O'Connell, and Jean Kelly – and to Anja and Christoph Henschel (Proprietors of Rose Bay General Store), Elroy and Betty Creaser, the late Charlotte Corkum, George and Janet Walker, Kevin and Suzanne Creaser,

Captain Douglas Himmelman and Louise Strickland, Charlotte and Keith Boates, David Tanner, Harry Conrad, Dwayne Porter (Railway Museum, Lunenburg), Philip Spenser, Beth Spindler, Bill and Susan Shaw, the late Captain Cecil Ritcey, Cornelis deVries, my brother George and sister Carolyn (Brown), cousins Faye (Spindler) Aiken, Norman Mossman, and Gerald Mossman, Lynn Mossman, Rachel Bailey, former Mayor of Lunenburg, Adrian Morrison, Curator of the Fisheries Museum of the Atlantic, Lunenburg, and staff members Hilda Russell, Daveda Savory, and Dwight Eisenhauer. Thanks to Scotland's so aptly named First Minister, Nicola Sturgeon, who helped me secure the delightful photograph of Queen Elizabeth II and company with Captain Leary's sturgeon.

Special thanks goes to Margaret Jean Layng, daughter of Arthur Benjamin Lohnes (AB) and Carrie Lenora, who encouraged me throughout this exercise, and to Ralph Getson, revered former Curator of the Fisheries Museum of the Atlantic, Lunenburg, who provided invaluable advice on a wide range of subjects as well as tape recordings of stories told by Aubrey Backman and Amos Crouse, and of an interview by Laurie Meister with Carmen Creaser.

Works Consulted

Bacon, John U. (2017). *The Great Halifax Explosion*. New York, NY: Harper Collins.

Barry, Sebastian. (2006). *The Secret Scripture*. New York, NY: Penguin.

Boileau, John. (2007). *Historic Eastern Passage*. Halifax, NS: Nimbus Publishing.

Boileau, John. (2017). *6:12:17 – The Halifax Explosion*. Halifax, NS: MacIntyre Purcell.

Boutilier, Alex D. (2014). *From 14th Colony to Confederation, 1749-1867. Governors, Placemen and the Merchant Elite*. Halifax, NS: New World Publishing.

Cahill, Bette. (1992). *Butterbox Babies*. Toronto, ON: Seal Books, McClelland-Bantam Inc.

Coggon, Allan. (2004). *Watch and Warn – a Wartime Story of Canada's Home Front – The Aircraft Detection Corps*. Victoria, BC: Trafford Publishing.

Creighton, Norman. (1998). *Talk About the Maritimes*. Halifax, NS: Nimbus Publishing.

Csikszentmihalyi, Mihaly. (1996). *Creativity: Flow and the Psychology of Discovery and Invention*. New York, NY: Harper Collins.

Cusack-McVeigh, Holly. (2017). *Stories Find You – Places Know*. Salt Lake City, UT: The University of Utah Press.

Cuthbertson, Brian. (1996). *Lunenburg: An Illustrated History*. Halifax, NS: Formac Publishing.

Cuthbertson, Brian. (2002). *Lunenburg Then and Now*. Halifax, NS: Formac Publishing.

DeMont, John. (2017). *The Long Way Home*. Toronto, ON: McClelland and Stewart.

DeVilliers, Marq and Sheila Hirtle. (1975, January 11). "The Other End of the Road." Weekend Magazine, *The Montreal Star*.

Dickson, Frances Jewel. (2007). *The DEW Line Years: Voices from the Coldest Cold War*. Lawrencetown Beach, NS: Pottersfield Press.

Dickson, Frances Jewel. (2008). *Skipper: The Sea Yarns of Captain Matthew Mitchell*. Lawrencetown Beach, NS: Pottersfield Press.

Elsworth, William B. "The Halifax Refinery." *The Imperial Oil Review*. Vol. II, No. 7 (July 1918): 3-5.

Graham, Genevieve. (2015). *Tides of Honour*. New York, NY: Simon and Schuster.

Greenblatt, Stepthen. (2011). *The Swerve: How the World Became Modern*. New York, NY: W.W. Norton & Co. Ltd.

Gutkind, Lee. (2012). *You Can't Make This Stuff Up*. Boston, MA: Da Capo Lifelong Books.

Hadley, Michael, L. (1985). *U-Boats Against Canada*. Kingston, ON, and Montreal, QC: McGill-Queens University Press.

Hallowell, Gerald. (2013). *The August Gales: The Tragic Loss of Fishing Schooners in the North Atlantic, 1926 and 1927*. Halifax, NS: Nimbus Publishing.

Himmelman, Mary Edith. (1978). *A Good Name*. Unpublished manuscript.

James, Terry. (1991). *Lunenburg County*. Halifax, NS: Nimbus Publishing.

James, Terry and Plaskett, Bill. (1996). *Buildings of Old Lunenburg*. Halifax, NS: Nimbus Publishing.

Kaulback, Ruth, E. (1970). *Historic Saga of Lehève (LaHave)*. Halifax, NS: Self-published.

Kurson, Robert. (2004). *Shadow Divers*. New York, NY: Random House.

Lohnes, Maxwell. (ca. 2008). *Captains of Lunenburg County*. Lunenburg, NS: Fisheries Museum of the Atlantic. Unpublished manuscript.

Major, Kevin. (2001). *As Near to Heaven by Sea: a History of Newfoundland and Labrador*. Toronto, ON: Penguin Canada.

McKee, Fraser, M. (2004). *"Sink all the Shipping there": The wartime loss of Canada's merchant ships and fishing schooners*. St. Catherines, ON: Vanwell Publishing Ltd.

Mosher, Jean. (ca. 1970). *Home Town Recipes of Riverport and District*. Riverport, NS: Ladies Auxilliary.

Oickle, Vernon. (2018). *I'm Movin' On: The Life and Legacy of Hank Snow*. Halifax, NS: Nimbus Publishing.

Parker, Mike. (1992). *Woodchips and Beans – Life in the Early Lumber Woods of Nova Scotia*. Halifax, NS: Nimbus Publishing.

Parsons, Robert. (1993). *Wake of the Schooners: From Placentia to Port aux Basques*. St. John's, NL: Creative Publishers.

Pope, William. (2006). *The Best of Wilfred Grenfell*. Halifax, NS: Nimbus Publishing.

Public Archives of Nova Scotia. (1967). *Place Names and Places of Nova Scotia*. Nova Scotia Series III. Halifax, NS: Public Archives of Nova Scotia.

Pugsley, William G. (1930). *Handbook on Reparation*. Ottawa, ON: Department of the Secretary of State, Reparations Branch.

Robinson, Cyril and Beaver, Bert. (1953, June 30). "Blue Water Family." Vol. 3, No. 25. Weekend Magazine, *The Montreal Star*.

Soucoup, Dan. (2017). *Explosion in Halifax Harbour – 1917*. Halifax, NS: Nimbus Publishing.

Snow, Hank. (1994). *The Hank Snow Story*. Chicago, IL: Board of the Trustees of the University of Illinois.

Stewart, Anthony and Terence Quincy Stewart. (1967). *The Ulster Crisis: Resistance to Home Rule 1912-1914*. London, UK: Faber & Faber.

Vicountess Byng of Vimy. (1946). *Up the Stream of Time*. Toronto, ON: The MacMillan Company of Canada Ltd.

Wentzell, Mary Permilla. (1910). *A Brief History of Riverport, N.S.* Unpublished manuscript.

Books by David Mossman

Going Over
A Nova Scotian Soldier in World War I

Titus Mossman fought with the 85th Canadian Infantry Battalion (Nova Scotia Highlanders). He earned the Military Medal at Amiens and a commendation for his actions at Drury. Against an overview of trench warfare, the campaigns undertaken by the 85th Battalion unroll. At war's end Titus is one of about a hundred "old originals" in his battalion, which started out as 1,115 soldiers. *Going Over* blends social, political, and historical issues of those turbulent times with the story of one young Canadian turned soldier, caught at the sharp edge of history. It also tells the costs of war and the after-effects on soldiers, their families, and succeeding generations.

Oceans of Rum:
The Nova Scotia Banana Fleet in Rum-Runner Heaven

Excitement, camaraderie, drama on the high seas, love affairs, big payoffs, fast cars – these were the returns for a life of smuggling in Atlantic Canada during Prohibition for those who dared. David Mossman's uncle Teddy, Captain Winfred "Spinny" Spindler, certainly dared. Like many others, the former deep-sea fisherman seized the opportunity to use his sea-going skills for rum-running between 1923 and 1938. Captain Spindler matured and endured through necessity, hard work, and tragedy, toward the end perservering like proverbial Job through his alloted ninety-three years.

Random Shots
Cheating Death and Embracing Danger:
Nova Scotia to Nunavut, Africa to Australia

In his globe-trotting memoir, David Mossman tells his stories of survival against the odds, the life of a well-travelled risk-taking Maritime son. Fortunate to have survived numerous near misses during the lead up to his eightieth trip around the Sun, he has much to be grateful for along the paths taken to adventure,

The Legend of Gladee's Canteen:
Down Home on a Nova Scotia Beach

This is the story of a popular Nova Scotia beach and a family who constructed a simple canteen at Hirtles Beach in 1951 and ran it for forty years. At the centre were Gladee and her sister Flossie, supported by the extended Hirtle family. Gladee's Canteen, several times voted one of the ten best restaurants in Canada, was a special example of co-operative and communal spirit. The era of Gladee's Canteen is a remarkable story that takes place in a small coastal Nova Scotia community blessed with a spectacularly dynamic living beach. In its time, the Hirtle family and its sparkling enterprise thrived in spite of relative isolation, uncertain funding, and domestic demons. As a Nova Scotia epic, the success story of Gladee's Canteen mirrors the recent history of Hirtles Beach, exemplifying the twists and turns locked up in legend.